KA 0039763 6

RIPEN OUR DARKNESS & THE DEVIL'S GATEWAY

Ripen Our Darkness and *The Devil's Gateway* are two bitingly funny political plays by feminist playwright Sarah Daniels, author of the controversial *Masterpieces*.

Ripen Our Darkness was premiered at the Royal Court Theatre Upstairs in 1981. 'Mary's farewell note to David, her churchwarden husband in Potters Bar, reads "Your dinner and my head are in the oven." A life of drudgery . . . has driven her to suicide and a celestial meeting with a wholly feminist trinity. En route, though, Mary scores two personal victories: she comes to terms with her daughter's lesbianism and sees off the absurd diagnostic stuttering of a doctor David has sent round to commit her to hospital . . . This rough-cut scenario of role-playing musical chairs and outlandish social comment marks a most promising debut and gives off the unmistakable aroma of new talent.' Michael Coveney, *Financial Times*

'Cascade of bile' Milton Shulman, *Standard*

'*Ripen Our Darkness* contains some of the best writing I've seen about women in our time.' Nick Dear, *Leveller*

The Devil's Gateway, premiered at the Royal Court Theatre Upstairs in 1983, 'is gloriously funny but the script deals with considerably more than dispatches from the home front on the battle between downtrodden Betty and her domineering husband Jim. Sarah Daniels has written a moving and true account of the consciousness raising of a working-class woman in Bethnal Green who has spent a lifetime mopping up after redundancy, unemployment and children. Betty's story could well be the story of any of the ordinary women who have left husbands and families to join the women's peace camps . . . Ms Daniels' strength lies in her ability to write comically but incisively about the lives of women and to prove that the personal is political. I left the theatre thinking about myself, my own mother, a little saddened and greatly uplifted.' Lyn Gardner, *City Limits*

'A sense of total, hilarious authenticity.' Irving Wardle, *Times*

WITHDRAWN FROM
THE LIBRARY

D1494159

The front cover shows Gwen Taylor as Mary in Ripen Our Darkness. *(Photo: John Haynes)*

by the same author

MASTERPIECES

RIPEN OUR DARKNESS

&

THE DEVIL'S GATEWAY

SARAH DANIELS

METHUEN · LONDON AND NEW YORK

A METHUEN PAPERBACK

First published in 1986 as a Methuen Paperback original
by Methuen London Ltd., 11 New Fetter Lane, London EC4P 4EE
and Methuen Inc, 29 West 35th Street, New York NY 10001
Copyright © 1986 by Sarah Daniels

Set in IBM 10 point Press Roman by 🅰 Tek-Art, Croydon, Surrey
Printed in Great Britain

British Library Cataloguing in Publication Data
Daniels, Sarah
   Ripen our darkness; & The devil's gateway.
   I. Title   II. Daniels, Sarah. Devil's gateway
   822'.914   PR6054.A52/

   ISBN 0-413-41140-0

CAUTION
These plays are fully protected by copyright. All rights are reserved and all enquiries
concerning the rights for professional or amateur stage productions should be made
to Judy Daish Associates, 83 Eastbourne Mews, London W2 6LQ (professional) and
Samuel French Ltd, 52 Fitzroy Street, London W1P 6JR (amateur). No performance
may be given unless a licence has been obtained.

This paperback is sold subject to the condition that it shall not, by way of trade or
otherwise, be lent, resold, hired out, or otherwise circulated without the publisher's
prior consent in any form of binding or cover other than that in which it is published,
and without a similar condition including this condition being imposed on the
subsequent purchaser.

KING ALFRED'S COLLEGE
WINCHESTER

822.9,
DAN   1112

RIPEN OUR DARKNESS

Ripen Our Darkness was first presented at the Royal Court Theatre Upstairs, London, on 7 September 1981, with the following cast:

MARY		Gwen Taylor
ANNA	⎞	
SUSAN	⎬	Cecily Hobbs
TARA	⎠	
DAPHNE	⎱	Janette Legge
RENE	⎰	
JULIE		Carole Harrison
DAVID	⎱	David Calder
ALF	⎰	
PAUL	⎞	
ROGER	⎬	John Gillett
MARSHALL	⎠	

Directed by Carole Hayman
Designed by Mary Moore
Lighting by Steve Whitson

Scene One

MARY's *kitchen, Sunday morning. She has just made tea. Presently* DAVID *enters, wearing a dressing-gown over a shirt and tie.*

DAVID: Good morning, dear, although that greeting seems almost inappropriate now, it being approximately nine fifty-five.

MARY (*flustered*): I can't believe it. Fancy sleeping through the alarm.

DAVID: Even if you had managed to wake up when it went, it was set for seven-thirty so we'd be half an hour behind already.

MARY (*confused*): But David, I'm sure that I set it for seven.

DAVID (*kindly*): Never mind. We've obviously both got to try to make up for lost time.

MARY: What would you like for breakfast?

DAVID: Oh, anything. (*He crosses to the window.* MARY *gives him a cup of tea.*) Thank you. Well, would you look at that. This is the day that the Lord hath made, and very beautiful it is too. The sort of day that makes you glad to be alive. And that reminds me, Mary, I don't like to mention it but it took me almost seven minutes to locate my underpants this morning.

MARY: Second drawer, dear. Will toast and cereal be all right?

DAVID: I know that now. Bacon and egg would go down well, but toast will suffice. (*He speaks kindly.*) And perhaps next time you reorganise the bedroom you would leave me a little plan or map as a guide, then I might be able to negotiate my way around the furniture, ha, ha. Maybe we could have a photo, ha, ha, then we'd be halfway to a National Trust booklet.

MARY: But David, they've been in the second drawer for the last thirty years.

DAVID: While you're there a couple of tomatoes would be nice. I'm sure they could not have been there that long, dear.

MARY: I remember distinctly re-lining that chest of drawers on Remembrance Sunday, 1950.

DAVID: Goodness me, you mean to say that with the war still fresh in our memories, you spent its fifth anniversary sorting underwear?

MARY: I did stop for two minutes.

DAVID: I should hope so. Well, no matter, it's of very little consequence now. What I meant to say is, perhaps when you have a minute you could enlighten me as to the whereabouts of my trousers.

MARY (*not listening*): I wonder how many minutes' silence we'll have to observe after nuclear war. . . .

DAVID: Really, dear, your sense of humour is quite macabre. But unfortunately it does not get me any further in the quest for my trousers.

MARY (*weary*): Where did you take them off?

DAVID: Ah ha, now that theory is good for as far as it goes. However, if I were to follow it through to its logical conclusion it would imply that they should be by the side of the bed where I stepped out of them.

MARY: They're folded on the back of the chair.

DAVID: Far be it from me, dear, but if you persist in allowing yourself to indulge in this rather morbid train of thought, how do you hope to get lunch organised in time for church?

MARY: But David . . .

DAVID: We don't want to start the day off with 'buts', now do we?

MARY: I don't think I'll be able . . .

DAVID: Now please, let's not start that

nonsense. It looks dreadful if you, of all people, aren't there. For goodness' sake, if the church warden's wife isn't able to come to church how do you expect us to reach the masses of Potter's Bar?

MARY: It's just that . . .

DAVID: And remember what we agreed, eh? What we worked out about being methodical, and getting things sorted out in a logical order so that it will give you more time to do things, to get important things fitted into the day. Especially Sunday.

MARY: Yes, David, I am trying.

DAVID: I know you are, I know. And this morning I'm going to help you out by getting the breakfast. How's that for men's lib, eh? Now, you sit down there. (MARY *sits absorbed*.) Well, you needn't look so grim about it.

MARY (*she has not heard*): Sorry, dear?

DAVID: I said, no need to be so glum.

MARY (*trying hard to please*): Oh no, it's very sweet of you. Thank you.

DAVID: And so to the gas.

DAVID *goes to the cooker.*

MARY: It's just that we're a bit behind anyway, and you've got a busy day ahead.

DAVID: That's precisely why I'm giving you a hand. Hmm, the gas doesn't seem to want to light.

MARY: Oh, no, I'm sorry, I forgot. You'll have to use the matches. The cooker's so old. I did ask . . .

DAVID: Don't tell me, it hasn't worked since the first Remembrance Sunday.

MARY: Strange really. I was always surprised that they didn't take it to turn into ammunition.

DAVID: Next step bacon. Where might that be?

MARY: In the fridge, dear.

DAVID: Ah ha, coming on in leaps and bounds. (*He looks in the fridge.*) Sorry, there appears to be no evidence of it here.

MARY: Second shelf, on the right, next to the half-eaten trifle.

DAVID (*removing the contents of the fridge item by item*): No, I'm sorry, dear, I'm prepared to say that it's not here.

MARY (*gets up slowly*): There, dear. (*She takes the bacon from the fridge and hands it to him.*)

DAVID: Now I was blowed if I could see it.

MARY (*cheerfully*): I'll do it, David . . . Please.

DAVID: The best-laid schemes and all that. Ah, well, don't say I didn't try.

MARY: Did you hear Simon come in last night?

DAVID: Considering the time, I think we should scrap the egg and bacon idea or I won't have room for lunch. A piece of toast, Mary.

MARY: Look at this mess. These plates. They come in at all hours, help themselves to something, I do wish they'd be a little more considerate.

DAVID: Boys will be boys, and they're not going to get any better if you persistently nag them, now are they?

MARY: I wouldn't mind, but Simon's twenty-three now.

DAVID: Goodness me, dear, we're not going to get very far if we keep nattering. Now, where's your pen and paper? I find things never seem so insurmountable if they're made into a list. For example, it will be easier to sort out the underwear drawer more than once in three decades, eh? Ha ha.

MARY: Pardon?

DAVID: Just a little joke, dear. Now, let me get those trousers on. What would

Roger think if he knew his church warden was still prancing about in his dressing-gown at ten-thirty on a Sunday morning, that's what I'd like to know.

DAVID *goes out.*

MARY (*sits down, starts to write*): Sunday. One, Dinner. Pick mint from garden for peas. Take cheesecake out of freezer . . . (*She looks up at the clock.*) Too late, it will never thaw. (*She continues writing.*) Tinned fruit and ice cream for pudding, cheesecake for tea. (*She stops writing.*) What about supper? I must be getting old, running out of imagination. (*She recommences writing.*) Dear God, why have I come to dread Sundays?

PAUL *enters.*

PAUL: Morning, Mum.

MARY (*startled*): Morning, dear. At least you're up.

PAUL: What's for breakfast?

MARY: Not long till lunchtime. Can't you hold out?

PAUL: Not really, no. How long's dinner anyway?

MARY (*brightly*): Four inches — it's a sausage.

PAUL: Please don't try to be funny, Mummy. It doesn't suit you.

MARY: Sorry. There's plenty of cereal in the cupboard.

PAUL: What sort?

MARY: Go and have a look.

PAUL: I won't bother then.

MARY *gets a bowl of cereal and gives it to* PAUL.

PAUL: Where's the milk?

MARY (*puts milk and sugar in the bowl of cereal*): There you are, dear.

PAUL: Ta, Ma.

MARY: Did you hear Simon come in last night?

PAUL (*stuffing his face*): Nope.

MARY: I don't think he came home last night. I haven't had a chance to look in his bedroom.

PAUL: He's a big boy now. A man of the world.

MARY: Even men of the world meet with fatal accidents. How would it look, 'Church warden's son run over and killed three days ago — his mother never even noticed'?

PAUL: Give it a rest, Mum.

MARY: I give up with you lot. Where's John?

PAUL: Judging by the sound of creaking bed springs coming from his room, I'd say he was reading magazines.

MARY: What on earth . . . Sometimes I can't follow a word you boys are saying. (*She shouts.*) John! Are you up? (*Then:*) Tut, they just ignore you. I don't know.

PAUL: Mum . . . I was wondering, could you see your way clear to lending me a fiver?

MARY: You mean give.

PAUL: It's difficult Mum . . . I mean . . .

MARY: You go out to work. I lent you five pounds out of the housekeeping last week. What did you do with that?

PAUL: Oh, you know, I mean, it's not like the day when you could buy a pound of apples for a penny.

MARY: And when was the last time you bought a pound of apples? Here, you're not on drugs, are you?

PAUL (*laughing*): At a fiver a week, I couldn't even afford to be on Smarties.

MARY: There's five pounds in the drawer.

PAUL: Ta.

MARY: Don't you think you can get off

that lightly. The washing-up, please.

PAUL: Ah . . . Mummy?

MARY: Who left all this out last night?
That's what I'd like to know.

PAUL: Oh, Ma, give over. Stop going on
for once, first thing in the morning,
it's too much.

MARY: Perhaps next time you could
wash up after yourself.

PAUL (*already halfway through the
door*): Shut up, will you? You old bag.

MARY: PAUL!

PAUL *goes out.*
DAVID *enters.*

DAVID: Not nagging him already, dear.
(*He shouts.*) Morning, son!

PAUL (*off*): Wotcher, Dad.

DAVID: Mm, something smells good.

MARY: Well, I don't know what. I
haven't had a chance to put anything
in the oven yet.

DAVID: Not to worry. Plenty of time,
eh? That's the idea. Now I hate to
mention it, but (*He points to his
trousers.*) that stain on the knee is
still there.

MARY: Sorry. I couldn't get it out. I'll
have to take them to the dry cleaner's.

DAVID: Don't be too rash, ha ha.

MARY: Pardon?

DAVID: I'm sure taking them to the dry
cleaner's will be the great event of the
week. Only a little quip. Hmm, yes
well. Now, I really must be going. I
suppose the car keys are in Paul's
room. And you will make an effort
to be at the service, won't you, dear?

DAVID *goes out.*

MARY (*shouts*): John, if you're not
down here in one minute . . . please.

PAUL *enters.*

PAUL (*putting head round the door*): By
the way, is it okay if I bring a bird
home with me tonight?

MARY: I suppose you mean a girl.

PAUL: I don't mean a sparrow, do I?

MARY: You know your friends are
always welcome here. Only I don't
want you spending too much time in
the bedroom. Whatever would people
think?

PAUL: Okay. Okay.

MARY: Now just a minute . . . I want
you to take these shirts upstairs for
me. (*She counts the shirts.*) I must be
going mad. Thirty-eight shirts for one
week, between four men. Fancy
wearing more than one shirt a day.
(*She hands the shirts to* PAUL.) Daft.
The whole lot of you.

PAUL: All right, Mum. I don't know
whose is whose, so you'll have to sort
them out later. I'll leave them on your
bed.

MARY: Thank you, dear.

PAUL *goes out.*
DAVID *enters.*

DAVID: Mary, you'll have a word with
that lad. I found something in his
room which I am far from pleased
about.

MARY: Oh.

DAVID: It's disgusting. Look!

*He opens his hand just long enough for
the audience to register that it is a
used condom.* MARY *does not take it
in.*

On his floor. I'll not have it.

MARY: No, it is a bit much.

DAVID: A bit much.

MARY: What will you do with it?

DAVID: Burn it.

MARY: That's a bit cruel.

DAVID *gets an envelope out of the
drawer, puts the condom in it, seals
it and puts it in his pocket.*

DAVID: What do you suggest I do?
Frame it? And while we're on about

the sordid part of this family, you and I really must have a talk about Anna.

MARY: Oh, good. I'll drop her a line this evening if I get a chance. You know, I can't tell you how much I miss her.

DAVID: She's a disgrace.

MARY: David!

DAVID: We'll have a long chat about it later.

MARY: Yes.

DAVID: Oh, and there, I almost forgot to tell you, I've invited Roger and Daphne back after the morning service.

MARY: Oh, that's nice. (*Slight pause.*) They won't want anything to eat will they?

DAVID: No, just lunch and tea.

DAVID *goes out.*

MARY: Oh. (*She continues writing.*) Tell Paul — no slugs in the bedroom. Two extra for lunch. Peel more potatoes. More sausages, to make the chicken go further. (*Pause.*) Why does my life seem like a half-finished jigsaw while everybody else seems to have completed their pictures? What did he mean about Anna? Dear God, if our lives are predestined what's the point of prayer? (*Pause.*) Even if they are not, what's the point?

Blackout.

Scene Two

RENE*'s kitchen.* ALF *is drunk.* SUSAN *sits silently at the table.* RENE *buzzes around frantically, dusting and polishing the tatty furniture. She is a nervous, agitated woman with a frail, frightened voice, which seems to be about to break into a more hysterical pitch.*

ALF (*at* SUSAN): Bleedin' slut. Cow. Little filthy fucker. See, yer know what this bleedin' is, eh? Retribution from God. All-bleedin' mighty. Mighty

wrath of God lands you with a shitty, vegetating baby. Thank fuck Christ it's dead. (*He lifts his hand to hit* SUSAN.)

RENE (*thin screech*): Steady, Alf, there's no need. Your dinner's almost ready. Toad in the hole, your favourite. I've managed to get the sausages you like — plenty of pork. The butcher was only saying . . .

ALF: Shut your stupid fucking gob.

RENE: He doesn't mean it. He's just upset. He's hurt. It's upset him more than we'll ever know. He doesn't mean it.

ALF (*shaking* SUSAN): You cow. You fuckin' wretched whore. Blasted fuckin' bitch, you reduced the whole fuckin' family to humiliation, you stupid ignorant slut.

RENE: Please, Alf. All she's been through. I know . . . maybe they got the babies mixed up at the hospital. A mistake. These things can happen, yer know. That's probably it.

ALF: You bleedin' fuckin' stupid bitch. Can't you shut that fuckin' blabberin' cake-hole for one fuckin' minute before I shuts it permanently for you?

The doorbell rings.

RENE: My God, who can that be?

ALF (*pokes* SUSAN): Answer it, slut.

SUSAN *goes to the door and comes back with* ROGER.

RENE (*tidying herself*): Oh, hello, Vicar.

ROGER: Hello there . . .

ALF: 'lo Vicar.

ROGER (*smiles*): And you must be Susan.

RENE: Yes. Say hello to the vicar, Susan.

SUSAN: Hallo.

RENE: I know we haven't been to church recently like, Vicar, well ever. But we've had a lot on our plates and Alf here used to work nights, when he was employed like, and sometimes he had to work on a Sunday as well, I know that don't make it right, for one thing you're not supposed to work on the Sabbath . . .

ALF (*through gritted teeth*): Rene, my dear.

RENE: Sorry. Sorry. Ha! I do go on, don't I?

ROGER: I've come to offer my sincere sympathies about little Peter. I baptised him just before he was taken.

ALF: He needed more than that, with no disrespect, Vicar.

ROGER: I realise this must be a very difficult time for you all, especially for Susan, and sometimes there is simply no explanation for these things.

ALF: She's not married, Reverend, there's your answer. Sin of the flesh.

ROGER: I'm afraid that we don't believe God is that hard these days.

RENE: Can I offer you a cup of tea, Vicar, or something to eat? We was just about to 'ave dinner. There's plenty.

ROGER: Thanks, but I've already accepted an offer from my church warden. I really called round to say that if ever — and I don't believe in ramming religion down other people's throats — but if ever you feel that there is anything you'd like to discuss or if you need spiritual guidance, do pop round to the vicarage and if I'm not there my wife will always be willing to chat over a cup of tea. Or the church warden's wife, Mrs Johnson, is very homely.

SUSAN: You baptised Peter? . . . What does it mean? Did you try to bring him back to life?

ROGER: No, my dear, but it does mean that he will definitely partake of the life hereafter.

SUSAN: Oh.

ROGER: He will be in paradise. I can vouchsafe. Well, nice to see you all. I'm only sorry that it couldn't have been in happier circumstances.

RENE: Nice of you to call, Vicar, and we can't thank you enough. I'll see you out. (*They both go to the door.*) It was a terrible thing to happen. Tragic. But we're over the worst of it now. I hope.

ROGER: So do I. God be with you.

RENE: And you.

They both go out.

ALF (*to* SUSAN): Bring it back to life? You stupid, ungrateful cow.

RENE *enters.*

RENE: Well, it was nice of him to call.

ALF: Bleedin' irony of it. Poncing in here saying, 'I don't want to ram religion down other people's throats,' well that, unfortunately, happens to be what he's bleedin' paid for. Soddin' git, don't know what a bleedin' day's work is anyway. Fuck it, I'm off out.

RENE: What about your dinner?

ALF: I'll have it when I get back.

RENE: It'll be spoilt.

ALF: It'd bleedin' better not be, and for fuck's sake woman, clear this place up a bit — it's like a fuckin' shit pit.

ALF *goes out.*

RENE: It ain't right, you know, Susan. I don't care what you say. Naturally you're upset but we got to pick up the threads somewhere, and I for one ain't going to take this lying down. I'm so upset, we, we all are — oh, yes, even your father, although he'd never show it of course. We'll sue those doctors, and we'll start with that Dr Cart-bleedin' double-barrelled Wright-Smith. Probably his name was Smith, and he pinched the Cartwright bit off his wife. Well, it's the same the world over, men always pinch the best things off women, bleed 'em dry, and for another thing . . .

SUSAN (*quietly*): Please, Mum . . .

RENE: We never 'ad no handicap in this family, and as for completely . . . well so badly handicapped he died . . .

SUSAN: Totally fucked up.

RENE: Susan, don't say that. It's a something syndrome. I'm so sorry, love, but we knew it was going to happen and I s'pose it's better now than later, oh what am I saying? It's just too easy to go on blabbing about all for the best.

SUSAN: When the baby's funeral's over, you and me are going.

RENE: Where could I possibly go at my age? I know your father's not exactly gracious . . . downright hostile . . . but it's not his fault . . . He's done his best by you he has.

SUSAN: So I noticed. Sorry. Perhaps we'd both better have a chat with the vicar's wife.

RENE: You've got to be joking. She's a real loony, she is. Mrs Wallanger from number forty-five can see their garden from her place. She told me that while the organ plays 'All things bright and beautiful' that vicar's lady wife tramps through the garden, ripping the heads off the snowdrops, shouting, 'Die damn you, die.'

SUSAN: Mum — Mrs Wallanger's hearing aid would have exploded if it was powerful enough to pick up that from the tenth floor — (*Slight pause.*) By the way, I'm going to see Julie next week.

RENE: What for? She didn't even know he existed.

SUSAN: There's no need to be so criticising.

RENE: You know what I think of that young lady — that's the wrong word — that young hermaphrodite more like, well I hope you don't pick up no bad habits, that's all I can say. Take it from me, Susan, women like that are never 'appy, how can they be?

SUSAN: Not like we are then, eh, Mum?

RENE: I thought it would be different when we was rehoused to Potter's Bar. (*She speaks more softly.*) It's my fault. I talked yer outta the abortion — mother's are supposed to know best — only this one's a complete bloody flop.

SUSAN: Mum, it's nobody's fault. If only for a few days Peter was alive.

RENE (*rising hysteria*): Alive! Alive my arse, he was like a bit of squashed fruit. (*She slaps herself.*) Oh, for Christ's sake, shut up, Rene.

SUSAN: Mum, I love you.

RENE (*getting out hanky*): Oh, shit. (*Pause.*) There's nothing to keep you here now, love. You go.

SUSAN: And leave you alone with him? No way.

RENE: What would I have done if you'd been a boy?

SUSAN: You'd 'ave ter have done the laundry yourself for starters. (*She picks up the laundry basket.*) See yer later.

RENE (*starts reading from the back page of* Woman's Own *aloud*): Dear Mary Grant, My wife and I make love about five times a week, which suits me down to the ground, but she will insist on watching telly over my shoulder. I don't mind this so much, but she will keep one hand free so she can switch stations with the remote control.

Pause.
RENE *puts down the magazine.*

Dear Mary Grant, I have a husband who drinks all my money away. I have two jobs to try to give him enough so he doesn't feel the need to slap me and my daughter around, but I usually fail. I have to lie in piss-soaked sheets, as my husband wets the bed every night. My daughter's severely handicapped baby has just died and I just can't stop fuckin' talking. I have dreams of doing myself in. Please don't reply as my husband rips up my mail regardless.

Blackout.

Scene Three

ANNA *and* JULIE*'s kitchen.* ANNA *is knitting.* JULIE *is watching television.*

JULIE: What yer doing?

ANNA: Washing-up.

JULIE: Yer bleedin' knitting, ain't yer? Yer disgustin' pervert. Yer know what yer equivalent to, eh? A man exposin' himself in public.

ANNA: I'm not in public, but I'll go to the window and wave it out shouting, 'Get a load of this double ply,' if you like.

JULIE: Same difference. Same crime.

ANNA: Be quiet, you're missing the programme.

JULIE: It's finished.

ANNA: Haven't you got an essay or something to write?

JULIE: Yeah. I've done it.

ANNA: Already?

JULIE: Here.

She hands ANNA *a postcard.*

ANNA (*reading*): Open University, Milton Keynes.

JULIE: Other side, Rubberhead.

ANNA (*turns it over, reads*): 'Dear madam, and if there is not a woman on the premises don't bother to read any further. I am writing to inform you that I cannot respond to any essay title with the word "mankind" in it. Because it has the kind of alienating effect which really fucks me off.'

JULIE: What do you think?

ANNA: You can't start a sentence with 'because'.

JULIE: Do you think it's long enough?

ANNA: For you it's almost a thesis.

JULIE: Hey, that reminds me, what did your mother have to say this week?

ANNA: What did my mother have to say this week?

She hands JULIE *a letter.*

Here, read it for yourself.

JULIE (*reads*): 'Dear Anna, sorry I can't write much as I have to get on with the beds, love Mum.' (*She looks up.*) That's it? Blimey, the Post Office should've let her have a stamp half price fer that.

ANNA: I just don't know what to make of it.

JULIE: Are you sure you didn't upset her when you went home?

ANNA: Yes, at least, I don't think so. It's difficult to tell, he puts her on edge so much.

JULIE: Who?

ANNA: The old bastard.

JULIE: Oh, Flash Gordon, the church warden.

ANNA: Sometimes I feel my visits cause more trouble than they're worth.

JULIE: Did you get a chance to speak to her on her own?

ANNA: Yes, but she's . . . I don't know. I can't explain it.

JULIE: She's been bullied so long she don't know how to pick herself up again.

ANNA: Yes, but my father has never so much as raised his hand to her.

JULIE: So what exactly did you say to her?

ANNA: Nothing really. I thought it would

make things about a million times worse if I told her about me and you.

JULIE: A cop out.

ANNA: Not altogether. I said I'd always preferred women to men.

JULIE: Not bad. What did she reckon to that?

ANNA: She gave me a long, wistful, smile, 'Oh, do you, dear?' then, after a pause, she said 'To tell you the truth, so have I. Half the time I don't know what men are on about.'

JULIE (*shrugs*): No one can say you didn't try.

ANNA: How can you explain to somebody whose whole life is centred around God and the family that our relationship is justifiable, let alone natural?

JULIE: Cause it is, it's nature's contraceptive. I'm sure we wasn't meant to be bored to death.

ANNA: Oh great, I'll tell her that.

JULIE: It ain't up to us to tell her she's wrong.

ANNA: What? That's what the Liberals said about Hitler.

JULIE: Oh, I give up.

ANNA: Hang on, is this the same person who had to be physically removed from the pub last night, screaming 'Off with their rocks!'?

JULIE: So? So?

ANNA: So? Half of my colleagues were there.

JULIE: Do you want to live a lie?

ANNA: That's not fair. They all know I'm gay.

JULIE: Gay? You're the most humourless, miserable fucker this side of the Blackwall Tunnel.

ANNA: All I know is that half the contents of the staffroom were making a valid point that all men go through the same shitty system as us, and your only positive contribution was to bang your fist on the table and shout, 'Off with their rocks.'

JULIE: Oh, yeah. I suppose, according to you, we should all go round cuddling rapists to make them more lovable human beings?

ANNA: No, but . . .

JULIE: Off with their rocks!

ANNA: I am honoured to have witnessed such a conversion in your personality. In the days when I first met you, you were a feminist with a few lesbian tendencies. Then you became a lesbian with a few feminist tendencies, to a radical revolutionary terrorist feminist, to a lesbian fuckwit.

JULIE: Am I still allowed to come to the school dance?

ANNA: Only if you can manage to keep from screeching out your obscenities. And this time you keep your lecherous thoughts to yourself.

JULIE: Bleedin' cheek, I ain't a man. Women don't feel lust.

ANNA: So what was the emotional force behind trying to get your leg over the secretary?

JULIE: Give over.

ANNA: Only you could fancy someone with seven kids and a husband in the police force.

JULIE: Fancy?

ANNA: Like 'be attracted to'.

JULIE: Oh, fuck me. What's a fancy got to do with anything? I don't try to look up women's skirts on escalators, or ogle the underwear ads, or shout 'Hello, darlin', what a nice pair you got,' after women in the street. (*She kisses* ANNA *on the ear.*) Oh, Anna, stop this bloody boring knitting.

ANNA: We've only just got up! Women don't feel lust, my arse.

JULIE: This is my insatiable lesbian persona.

ANNA: Okay. Let me finish this row.

JULIE: Blimey, I hope that's not the equivalent of, 'Not just at the moment, darling, I've got a headache.' Can't you do it another time?

ANNA: Some of us work at other times, or had you forgotten?

JULIE: I do the Open University.

ANNA: What are you on about? Women do feel lust.

JULIE: Right, but there's one main difference — you don't find women wanking each other off under toilet doors.

ANNA: A fact I can't deny.

JULIE: So what's the reason why?

ANNA: Because they'd break their wrists on the partitions.

JULIE: Are you deliberately trying to misunderstand me? You find blokes going into toilets, sucking off other blokes and walking off without giving it another thought.

ANNA: Shut up, will you?

JULIE: What's the matter?

ANNA: I'm worried.

JULIE: I know you don't like the Open University. I suppose I did take on a bit much.

ANNA: You didn't have to do all 392 degrees. You'll end up in the bin.

JULIE: Well, I s'pose I could drop the extra-mural course in aesthetics.

ANNA: No, I'm a bit worried about my mum.

JULIE: Did you tell her she could come and stay here?

ANNA: Yes. She looked at me as though I'd just suggested that she cut her head off.

JULIE: Your spaghetti bolognese does leave something to be desired.

ANNA: When I suggested that she should go to a women's group she laughed.

JULIE: That all?

ANNA: No, she said, 'What do they do then? Put their hand on a toadstool and say, "I promise never to stir my husband's tea again!" '

JULIE: You just gotta wait till she realises it for herself.

ANNA: I can't see that she'll ever do that.

JULIE (laughs): You are a patronising big-head.

ANNA: What made your mum aware of male supremacy then?

JULIE: My dad.

ANNA: It's not as if she's read the right books.

JULIE (explodes): What?! Do all teachers reek of elitist arrogance? Whoever learnt anything from a book?

ANNA: All right, all right, but how . . .

JULIE: Life's experience don't count for nothing, I s'pose.

ANNA: Well you didn't do so well with the step-mother.

JULIE: Fuck off.

ANNA: Nor your half-sister.

JULIE: We still keep in touch.

ANNA: Come off it, the last time you heard from her was about a year ago.

JULIE: For your information I got a note from her yesterday suggesting that we go for a drink.

ANNA: That still doesn't excuse your unsisterliness in leaving home without her.

JULIE: Anna — I was sixteen. She was eight. Radical as I am, I never envisaged setting up an alternative Dr Barnados.

ANNA: Why do you always have the last word?

JULIE: Because I ain't read the right books, thank God.

Blackout.

Scene Four

MARY's *kitchen.* MARY, DAVID, DAPHNE *and* ROGER *are playing Monopoly.*

DAPHNE: Really, David. That's not fair.

ROGER: Come off it, darling. That is a jolly good offer.

DAPHNE: You're joking. David, you're practically giving it away.

DAVID: Nonsense. No one can ever win with that set. I'll swop you Leicester Square for Bond Street, plus five hundred pounds.

DAPHNE: Done.

DAVID: And, Mary, I'll give you five hundred pounds for Regent Street. Mary, dear? Are you with us?

MARY (*vacant*): Sorry? Sorry, dear, what did you say?

DAVID: I said I'll buy Regent Street from you for for five hundred pounds.

MARY (*smiles*): That's all right, dear. You can have it.

DAPHNE: Mary, don't be daft.

DAVID: Try to play the game, dear. You'll never get anywhere unless you play to win.

MARY: Sorry, dear. It's just that I haven't caught up with the washing-up from lunch, and now the tea things . . .

DAVID: Don't worry about that, we'll all give a hand later. Now here's five hundred pounds.

MARY: Thank you.

DAVID: Besides, what were you doing while I was showing Daphne the rhododendrons?

MARY: Making the tea.

DAVID: I don't think we need contradict each other all of the time.

MARY: No, dear. I mean yes, dear.

ROGER: Where did you get all that money from, Daphne?

DAPHNE: From you landing on my property.

ROGER: You couldn't possibly have accumulated that lot.

DAPHNE: Some of us remember to collect two hundred pounds as we pass Go.

DAVID: Right. Now who wants houses?

ROGER: Six, please.

DAVID: Six houses at one hundred and fifty pounds, each, that's . . .

ROGER: Nine hundred pounds. There you go, old boy.

DAPHNE: Is David always the banker?

ROGER: Whoever heard of an Anglican church warden cheating at Monopoly on a Sunday? What's got into you, Daphne?

DAVID: Well, you see, Mary's got no money sense.

MARY (*vague*): Pardon? The housekeeping's not out, is it?

DAVID: No, silly. I meant that you have no business sense.

DAPHNE: Well, three hotels for me please, David.

ROGER: See what I mean? Where did you get that cash?

DAPHNE: It's only Pentonville and Euston Road, for Christ's sake . . . er, I mean, for goodness' sake.

ROGER: I'll pretend that I didn't hear that.

DAPHNE: Hey, Mary, you haven't got a set.

DAVID: Don't worry, Daphne. Mary's never been much of a one for getting into the spirit of things. Hasn't got my drive for excitement. Now, whose turn?

ROGER: Mine. Now then, let's see . . . who's this on Fleet Street? David. Right, Fleet Street with two houses, that's six hundred pounds.

DAPHNE: If we'd have taken Mary's advice in the first place and played to the nearest ten pounds we wouldn't have spent nearly two hours getting to the buying stage.

DAVID: Playing to the nearest ten pounds! Have you ever heard the like, Roger? Sacrilege. I ask you. Pure sacrilege. Well, Roger, you have my sympathy if Daphne plays to the nearest ten pounds with the housekeeping. Ha ha.

ROGER: Sorry, Mary, it looks like you've landed on me. Let me see, Trafalgar Square with two houses . . . That's six hundred pounds.

MARY: Oh, dear. Well, it looks as though I'm cleared out.

DAVID: Wait a minute now, let's see. If you mortgage the stations and the gas works, plus the cash . . .

MARY: It's hardly worth it. I'll make a start on the washing-up.

DAVID: Mary, you have no sense of competition.

MARY: But, dear, I . . .

DAVID: Oh well, a cup of tea would be nice, while you're up.

DAPHNE: Do let me help.

DAVID (*as* MARY *goes out*): She hates anyone under her feet, don't you dear? (*He sees her leaving the kitchen.*) Where are you going, Mary? What are you doing?

MARY (*as she re-enters*): I wanted to go to the lavatory first, David.

MARY *goes out.*

DAVID (*embarrassed*): Oh, sorry. There,

see what I mean? Very absent-minded.

DAPHNE: Well, for the short time we've known you, Mary has always seemed a, well, a vague sort of person.

DAVID: It's not so much that as this 'couldn't care less' sort of attitude. I told her you were coming, but she didn't even have anything ready. Time and again it's been the same. Last week there was a twenty-minute gap between the first course and the pudding. Time and time again.

ROGER: Come on, old boy, don't be too hard on Mary. She needs a jolly good rest, and what we talked about seems just the thing.

DAVID: I'm glad you agree. But I don't want her to think anything's wrong. (*To* DAPHNE:) Daphne, perhaps after we've had a cup of tea, you two could have a little chat while you help her with the washing-up.

DAPHNE: What about you?

ROGER: Come off it, if he insists on doing the washing-up it will give the game away.

DAPHNE: You're the one to talk, darling.

ROGER: We have our work cut out on Sundays as it is, don't we David? And, in the separate occupation Our Lord has chosen for us, all the other days of the week as well. How are things at the office at the moment, old boy?

DAVID: Fine, fine. You know.

ROGER: Actually, I was going to ask you . . .

DAPHNE: I meant, why don't you talk to her first?

DAVID: Difficult to say that sort of thing, you know women. Ask them what's wrong and they get annoyed.

DAPHNE: How will you cope if she does go away for a week?

DAVID: Oh, the lady next door is very good.

ROGER: And I'm sure that plenty of the lady parishioners will rally round.

DAPHNE: Well, I must say she does look tired.

ROGER: And David, you must try and remember . . .

DAPHNE: Damn . . . I mean, blow. I've left my cigarettes in the car.

DAVID (*trying hard not to appear shocked*): I didn't know you smoked.

ROGER: She's trying to give up, aren't you, Daphne?

DAPHNE: Yes, Roger, I'm trying.

DAPHNE *goes out.*

DAVID: Oh dear. I hope it wasn't anything I said.

ROGER: Goodness me no. What were we saying? Oh yes . . . Now you mustn't be too hard on Mary. Her role is not to be undermined and routine can prove to be quite boring from time to time, so I've heard.

DAVID: But I . . .

ROGER: Even when they're used to it. I know it's sometimes hard to remember, I should know, I'm the world's worst. Take Daphne . . . though I must say she's much better since I gave her the go-ahead with the Youth Club. You know what Mary needs? A sense of responsibility. Maybe she could help out with the Mother's Union . . .?

DAVID: I don't think . . .

ROGER (*patronising*): And it's not really up to us to speak for them. Believe it or not women have minds of their own. Ha ha! You know sometimes I forget that Daphne has a degree.

DAVID: Has she?

ROGER: Yes. Mind, it's only a two:one.

DAVID (*unsure*): Ah, of course.

ROGER: But it all adds up to the fact that we do have to tread a bit carefully with the fairer sex these days.

DAVID: Yes, I suppose . . .

ROGER: And don't forget, I can always get Marshall Hutchinson to drop in.

DAVID: Marshall Hutchinson?

ROGER: That old college pal of mine. You know. Works as a psychiatrist at the Royal and General. Most of his work is private, but I'm sure he'd make a home visit on the National Health if I said it was for a friend of mine.

DAVID: That's very kind.

ROGER: Anyway, it might not come to that. I'm sure Daphne will be able to cheer her up.

DAVID: Frankly, I'm beyond optimism.

ROGER: Nonsense. Women do each other a power of good. There's nothing they enjoy more than a good chat about depression.

DAVID: Believe me, Mary's about as alert as a ball of wool in the fog.

MARY *re-enters.*

DAVID: By the way, how did things go with that family this morning?

ROGER: Interesting. I'm very glad that estate is in the parish. Working-class people are so genuine.

DAVID: Salt of the earth. (*He looks down.*) Where's my tank?

ROGER: Here, use the shoe, old boy.

DAVID: No, I always have the tank. It's been a tradition in this family, from way back when we all used to play together as a family. I've always been the tank. It reminds me of the Church Army. Dear, have you seen the tank?

MARY: Where did you leave it?

DAPHNE *re-enters.*

DAPHNE: Your tank?

DAVID: On Fleet Street. Oh, dear me. It looks as if we'll have to abandon the game.

DAPHNE: Oh no, what a shame.

MARY *pours out the tea, using the milk straight from the bottle.*

DAVID: Mary, don't we use the milk jug anymore, dear?

MARY: Sorry, I forgot to tell you. It broke last week.

While MARY's *back is turned* DAVID *gives* DAPHNE *and* ROGER *a 'there-what-did-I-tell-you' look.*

DAVID: Really, Mary. That was a wedding present.

MARY: I'm sorry.

DAVID: Well, don't worry, never mind. Can't be helped. Accidents will happen.

ROGER: Oh, yes, I've remembered what I wanted to ask you about. Perhaps, we could do a chat or something on 'Numbers in the Congregation'. I think, since my arrival, I've got them down to thirty-two.

DAPHNE: Haw haw, my Roger is really quite a card.

ROGER: That reminds me, did you hear the one about the Catholic priest who was arrested for practising celibacy in the street?

They all laugh, including MARY *who doesn't understand it.*

DAPHNE: Always find that one hilarious. (*She mutters through clenched teeth.*) Just as well, I hear it every blasted day.

DAVID (*drily*): Oh, very good.

MARY (*absently*): But how . . . I mean, he couldn't have been doing anything . . .

The others laugh at her but not unkindly.

ROGER: Never mind. How are the boys these days, Mary?

MARY: Oh, fine, fine. I think. I mean, aren't they David?

DAVID: Oh yes, all's well there.

MARY: Well, we've had one or two little traumas, haven't we?

DAVID: Not now, dear. We won't go into that.

ROGER: Sounds interesting. I'm in the wrong profession. It's only the clergy who think the phrase 'miserable as sin' is accurate.

DAPHNE: Now then, Roger.

MARY *resumes pouring the tea, without noticing that she is pouring it into the sugar basin.*

DAVID: My dear, are you aware that you are pouring tea into the sugar basin?

MARY (*flustered and embarrassed*): Tut, oh silly me.

DAPHNE: Come on, Mary, let me help you with the washing-up and leave these two to compare parochial notes.

DAVID *and* ROGER *go out, carrying cups of tea.*

DAVID: Come along, Roger.

ROGER (*off*): Oh Daphne? Could you give me Marshall's number? I've forgotten it at the moment.

DAPHNE (*finds address book in bag*): Coming! I won't be a second, Mary.

DAPHNE *goes out.*

Slowly MARY *clears up the game of Monopoly. When she has finished she finds the missing tank, but does not immediately put it into the box with the rest of the game. Instead she picks up a rolling pin from the washing-up and strikes the tank with it.*

MARY (*with aggression*): The (*Bang.*) Church (*Bang.*) Army (*Bang.*) drives (*Bang.*) you (*Bang.*) barmy! (*Bang.*)

DAPHNE *enters.* MARY *hastily puts the tank and rolling pin away.*

DAPHNE: Oh good. Now we can have a chat, just you and I.

MARY: Was it planned?

DAPHNE: Haw, haw, I don't think so. You and I never get the chance to chat together, just the two of us. (*Slight pause.*) Yes?

MARY (*suspicious*): Hmm. Well, it's nice anyway.

DAPHNE: Is there anything on your mind, Mary?

MARY: No. That's just it, my mind seems empty.

DAPHNE: I really do think you should try and get away, even if it's only for a few days.

MARY: You're not very subtle about coming to the point.

DAPHNE: Sorry, was it obvious? Believe me, Mary, you look like you need a rest.

MARY: But what would happen to all this?

DAPHNE: I'm sure the do-good lady parishioners can manage something . . .

MARY: Yes, plenty — all too willing to have a nose round the church warden's home and criticise his wife, I can just hear them now . . . Oh, I'm sorry.

DAPHNE (*softly*): Don't be. You don't have to apologise to me for your feelings.

MARY (*pause*): Actually, I would love to go and see Anna.

DAPHNE: Your daughter? She's a teacher, isn't she?

MARY: That's right. I can't see that David wants me to go.

DAPHNE: I think that he only wants what's best for you. How he arrives at the conclusion that he knows what's best is perhaps another matter. Goodness, all that washing-up!

MARY: Yes. All these years and the washing-up after Sunday lunch still not fitted into the routine.

DAPHNE: Do you have a tea-towel?

MARY: Second drawer. How do you think you're settling into Potter's Bar?

DAPHNE: Oh Mary, it's awful here.

MARY: How do you mean?

DAPHNE: Oh, you know, the people round here like to keep themselves so much to themselves . . . Even the dogs are too shy to shit.

MARY: No, I can see you're not liking it. David says that I've never tried to mix properly.

DAPHNE: What does he know — stupid bag of poop.

MARY: Daphne? Do you ever get cross?

DAPHNE (*cheerfully*): Oh, only about twice a year — and then it only lasts for six months at a time.

MARY: Do you think I'm mad?

DAPHNE: No more than the rest of us. (*She adds quietly:*) Men are such bloody bastards.

MARY: Funny you should say that about men. When Anna was here she told me that she preferred women's company to men's.

DAPHNE: Don't we all, dear?

MARY: Only she seemed to think it was a big confession.

DAPHNE: Young people take themselves so seriously.

MARY: And I overheard Paul talking to her in the lounge . . . But I don't understand what anybody says any more.

DAPHNE: Well, what were they saying?

MARY: Paul said to Anna, 'You're a dyke.'

DAPHNE: What did Anna say?

MARY: Something about, 'It's been a long time since a little Dutch boy stuck his finger in me.'

DAPHNE: I see.

MARY: What?

DAPHNE: I think she meant that she prefers women's company in bed as well as out.

MARY: Oh. (*Then a long pause as she tries to digest this.*) Do you mean . . . I mean . . . Do they kiss?

DAPHNE: I should suppose so.

MARY: And touch each other?

DAPHNE: I would have thought so.

MARY: What on earth for?

DAPHNE: I don't know. (*She shrugs.*) Love?

MARY: No, she did say something, now I remember, about a political decision.

DAPHNE: Crumbs. I've heard of thinking about God, or the Queen, but the state of the economy? That's a bit hard to swallow. I would have assumed it was more of a biological thing.

MARY: Oh my. (*Pause.*) I always said that that antenatal care left a lot to be desired. (*Pause.*) Oh my. (*Pause.*) What a dreadful thing.

DAPHNE: Dreadful? Rubbish, it sounds jolly good fun.

MARY: Have you ever thought about it?

DAPHNE: Not as a rule. Certainly not when I'm fully clothed.

MARY: Daphne!

DAPHNE: Mary, how can it be wrong or dreadful if it just comes into your head naturally?

MARY: Well, sometimes, quite naturally, I have an idea that I want to kill someone.

DAPHNE (*shrugs*): We can't all be perfect, now can we? Now, I wonder what's happened to those frightfully hideous bores we married.

MARY: Daphne?

DAPHNE: Yes?

MARY: Have you . . . I mean, have you ever done it? With a woman?

DAPHNE: Goodness me, no. (*Slight pause.*) Not since I was at Millfield anyway.

DAVID *and* ROGER *enter.*

DAVID: Ha, there you are. (*He claps.*) Did you have a good chat?

DAPHNE: Yes, I think so. Mary was saying how much she'd enjoy a rest.

ROGER: Well it certainly seems to have brought the colour back to her cheeks.

MARY: I mean, if it's not . . . if it won't be too much trouble.

DAVID: Nonsense, dear. I think it's a wonderful idea.

DAPHNE: Cheerio, and thanks for the lunch and the tea.

DAPHNE *goes to kiss* MARY *on the cheek.* MARY *visibly stiffens and turns away.*

ROGER: Yes, absolutely great. Bye.

ROGER *and* DAPHNE *go out.*

DAVID: I must say I do think you've made the right decision. I know that you won't take offence if I tell you that you've been looking so worn out lately.

MARY: It will be nice to see Anna on her own. I'll drop her a note this evening.

DAVID: Anna? Oh, no, my dear, the less we see of that young madam the better. I've arranged for you to go on a retreat. Didn't Daphne explain?

MARY: Daphne explain? A retreat? David, what are you on about?

DAVID: It's a special conference for those women who are married to men involved in the Church. An opportunity for you to meditate and re-dedicate your life to the Lord and His works.

MARY: But David, I am already!

DAVID: You've suffered a lapse in attitude. For example, I see Daphne had to help you with the washing-up which was still left over from lunch.

MARY: But David, you insisted that I play Monopoly.

DAVID: And that's another thing, your reluctance to take part in family activities.

MARY: But, David.

DAVID: Don't worry.

MARY: But, David . . .

DAVID: There you go again, dear. I think your epitaph could be 'But David'. Let's have some Horlicks.

MARY: Are you sure you'll be able to cope?

DAVID: I think we can manage until you get back, ha ha. And I'm going to see this doctor friend of Roger's while you're away and have a long chat with him.

MARY: Are you ill?

DAVID: No dear, about you. You see, you're just so disorientated.

MARY: Daphne was very strange this evening. Did you know that she hates men?

DAVID: Hates men? What a way for a vicar's wife to behave. Between ourselves she's not very popular. Even the bishop said she was unhinged.

MARY: Well, she swore.

DAVID: Good grief. I don't think you need repeat it.

MARY: Oh, I wouldn't repeat it, but she said all men are . . . blank, blanks.

DAVID: Great Scott! Did she? Do you think we should warn Roger?

MARY: No, don't do that.

DAVID: Hmm. Sure you haven't been hearing things again? Now, are you coming to bed? We've an early start tomorrow.

MARY: Soon. I've got too much to do at present.

DAVID (*smiles*): Well, don't be too long. See you in a minute.

DAVID *goes out.*

MARY: Monday, dinner — beefburger, chips and peas. Tuesday, casserole, apple pie in freezer. Wednesday, fishcakes and . . . and . . . oh God, I don't want to go tomorrow, everyone will know I think rude words and that I'm decomposing from the inside . . . (*Slower:*) Dear God, why do people kiss? On reflection it seems so disgusting to put your mouth on somebody else's. Dear God, where do other people get the motivation for living from? (*She takes out the bible.*) Dear God, please give me some guidance. (*She opens the Bible, closes her eyes and sticks a pin in a passage at random. She reads the passage.*) 'And Judas went out and hanged himself.'

Blackout.

Scene Five

TARA. *Monologue.*

TARA: I don't believe you've met my husband, Marshall, yet. He's a psychiatrist. Yes, quite a conversation-stopper, isn't it? People are always intrigued to know about the ins and outs of his home life. You know, like the fascination we all have about clergymen who embezzle the collection or policemen who murder prostitutes, but unfortunately, Marshall's typically sane. Of course, he has his little routine and rituals. And as for sex, well, my dear, you can imagine how paranoid psychiatrists are about that. When we were first married we used to go to the Greek islands for our holidays and I adored making love on the beach but Marsh, poor love, was absolutely, obsessionally, preoccupied with the fear of getting a grain of sand under his foreskin. He thinks that magazines like *Forum* are where it's at. That's where he got the idea to try and train me to relax my throat muscles to perfect my fellatio performance. Don't misunderstand me, it's not that I don't enjoy risking my life but I do make it a little rule that I derive some pleasure from it. We've got two children and Marsh worked himself into a state of psychosis in case they were born with one testis too few or too many but despite all fears they're terribly normal. Oh, yes, they're both boys — pigs — don't tell me, darling, I've tried them with the handicraft classes, cookery, the lot, until I've literally pulled my hair out — still, I must be fair, they're not all bad. The youngest, he's eight, burnt the Scout hut down last week, so there's hope yet.

Of course, we have someone who takes the tedium out of housework — you know, our little treasure — does that sound exploitative? Frankly, I'm bored out of my mind and if I had to do irksome grotto chores I'd go completely off my head.

I love going to the pictures in the afternoon — it's so common.

Marshall is still trying to sue Ken Russell because it was after I saw *Women in Love* I suffered my little bout of kleptomania. Anyway, you know that bit in the film where that other woman smashes a vase over that prick's head — are we still allowed to say 'prick'? Are we still allowed to say 'head'? God, this modifying of manmade linguistics has got us all confused. Anyhow, to cut a long story short, I lifted a Baccarat paperweight from Liberty's. Quite what I had in mind I don't know but one of our solicitor friends got me off the hook by saying I'd had a bad day.

Between you and I, Marsh has begged me to divorce him. Why should I? I don't want to live in some pokey little flat where some social worker might try and certify me for being batty. No thanks. I like being posh.

Don't listen to this live without men rot. The way forward is to use them and have some fun.

Scene Six

The retreat.
   All the women sit in silence with cups of tea and Bibles on their laps. WOMAN ONE *discreetly tops up her tea with gin from a hipflask which is concealed in her pocket. Presently a* PRIEST *enters dressed in a purple robe.*

PRIEST: Good afternoon, ladies. I trust you enjoyed luncheon? (*There is a general response of smiles and nods.*) I would very much like to introduce you to Mrs Johnson who will be joining us this week. As you know we don't approve of the use of first names here, just in case it puts any little temptations in the way of our vow of silence. So, when you have finished your tea perhaps you'd go to your room for your continual confession and purification in solitude. We shall reconvene at 9 p.m. for our daily service of Holy Communion, before retiring to bed . . . um, er slumber . . . at nine-thirty.

The PRIEST *exits.*
Pause.

WOMAN ONE (*quietly, very slurred through excess of alcohol*): Holy Commune . . . Communion?

MARY (*leans over, confides in a whisper*): Eucharist.

WOMAN ONE: So would you be if you'd been here a frigging fortnight.

Gradually the women get up and go out in silence.

MARY (*to herself*): In all the time we've been married this is the first time I've spent a week away from David. I even had the last three children at home. I wonder if time on my own is what I need to find what is missing from my life. (*Pause.*) I wonder why I have always said 'not very well' instead of 'period'? And why . . . What am I saying? I am not here to indulge myself in obscene fantasies . . . Dear God, if you want me to recommit my life to your service please give me another, more appropriate sign. (*She opens her Bible, then looks up.*) But this is definitely the last chance you're getting. Otherwise there are going to be some drastic changes in this servant's life.

She shuts her eyes, puts her finger on a passage, then reads it aloud.

'Go thou and do likewise.'

Blackout.

Scene Seven

A week later, ANNA *and* JULIE's *kitchen.*

JULIE *is surrounded by hundreds of cassettes which she appears to be relabelling.* ANNA *is looking through a pile of children's exercise books, occasionally tutting and ripping out a page.*

JULIE: What are you doing?

ANNA (*absorbed in her own thoughts*): It's Open Day tomorrow.

JULIE: I know that, don't I? So what are you ripping up the books for?

ANNA: Because there are things in them that some of the parents aren't going to be overjoyed at seeing.

JULIE: What like? 'My teacher keeps a pin-up of Juliet Bravo on her desk lid'?

ANNA (*irritated*): Oh, you're so funny. (*She rips out another page.*)

JULIE: Let's have a look then.

She sits next to ANNA *and they read through a book together.*

ANNA: Here, look at this. (*Reading:*) 'Yesterday my Uncle Joe was drunk on the toilet floor and I had to step over him to have a shit.'

JULIE: Nice picture though . . . I wonder if they've really got a purple bathroom suite.

ANNA: This could be a good one. (*She looks at the cover and reads:*) 'Tracy Jones. News Book.' (*She continues reading:*) 'When my dad came home from the pub last night he smashed my mum up proper.' (*She says sarcastically:*) No, we don't say 'proper', Tracy, we say 'properly'. (*She rips out the page.*)

JULIE: Gawd, would you look at that picture. Wonder how much of our rates goes on red, black and blue felt-tips?

ANNA (*picking up another book*): 'Last night my daddy woke me up when he was doing things to my mummy.'

JULIE: Strange picture. Just a line?

ANNA: That's where I was looking over his shoulder and said in my best teacher's voice, 'No picture. Thank you, Darren.' And snatched the book away.

JULIE (*laughs*): That proves it, you are definitely prejudiced against heterosexuality, Miss Johnson. (*She writes on cassette cover.*) Wankers!

ANNA (*continuing to look through the exercise books*): Have you finished fucking up the OU cassette library?

JULIE: Yeah, I s'pose so.

ANNA: And what, dare I ask, did they think of your seminar?

JULIE: Which one?

ANNA: The one on birth control.

JULIE: They were bloody rude about it.

ANNA: Surprise, surprise.

JULIE: It was only s'posed to be a metaphorical piece, a point for discussion.

ANNA (*sarcastic*): I'm sure that your suggestion that birth control should be compulsory and used by men only went down a treat.

JULIE: Actually it did. Apart from that stupid reactionary woman who piped up from her Lentheric advert dream with, 'Oh, but I still enjoy men holding open the door for me.'

ANNA: Holding her legs open, more like.

JULIE: What's got into you?

ANNA: Nothing, sorry. So what went wrong?

JULIE: That hateful shit Nigel says, 'Oh yeah, and just what form might that take then, love?

ANNA (*helpfully prompting*): So you said, 'A pill, to be taken by men'?

JULIE: No, I said, 'A hand grenade held firmly between the knees.'

ANNA: Perhaps you should write a book on how to put people's backs up, or how to get on with members of the opposite sex without losing your looks.

JULIE: You got any ideas on what I can do my thesis on? It's got to be something I'm interested in.

ANNA (*sarcastic*): Oh, that shouldn't be too hard, considering you hate everything.

JULIE: I do not. At most there are only five things I actually hate.

ANNA: Yes. Art, travel, society, anything manmade, or anything alive. Oh, sod it. What in hell's name are we doing? You with your cranky sabotage of the Open University. They're only ordinary people trying to get on as best they can — they weren't born into it.

JULIE: What do you suggest I do, become a housemother at Eton?

ANNA: And me. What in fuck's name am I doing? Priding myself on pioneering non-sexist literature for use in my classroom.

JULIE: You didn't get a letter from your mum this week, did you?

ANNA: No.

JULIE: Judging from the last one, she probably wrote 'very busy' on the back of a stamp. Have you phoned?

ANNA: Yes, no answer.

JULIE: She could have gone out.

ANNA: She only goes shopping. I've rung every break-time for the past three days.

JULIE: Well, ring now.

ANNA: They'll be at church now. I'll ring a bit later.

JULIE: There's nothing you can do till then, so stop worrying.

The doorbell rings.

ANNA: Who the hell can that be?

I hope it isn't that Nigel, with instructions of where to put your hand grenade.

JULIE: Oh, God, you go and answer it in your teacher's voice.

ANNA *goes out.*
JULIE *picks up the exercise books and looks through them.*

ANNA (*off*): Mum!

ANNA *enters with* MARY.

ANNA: What's happened? What are you doing? Are you all right?

MARY: Of course, I'm all right. I just thought I would come and visit my daughter, but I can't . . .

ANNA: Good, you've left him.

MARY: No, I haven't left him. Honestly, love, what a thing to infer. I can't stop, this is just a flying visit. I only wanted to see how you are. (*To* JULIE:) Hello, you must be Anna's friend.

JULIE: Hello, you must be her mum.

ANNA: Oh, sorry, Mum, this is Julie. Julie, this is my mum.

MARY: Nice to meet you, Julie. Anna tried to tell me about you last week.

Pause.

But it didn't sink in at first.

JULIE: Oh, really . . .

Pause.

MARY (*sighing*): Well, I can see that I'm going to have to wait a long time before you two insist that you're just flatmates.

Pause.

Now I really can't stop long.

ANNA: Perhaps long enough to sit down? (*Pause.*) So how did you get here?

MARY: Oh, yes. (*She sits.*) Right, well it's quite a long story, but your father — no, it started before that, really . . . You know I'd been feeling a bit under the weather . . . Well, anyhow, your father thought it would be a good idea if I went away for a rest, and he packed me off on this — I don't know quite how to describe it — this get together of women married to men working for the Church, only nobody was allowed to talk or communicate in any way, no phone, nothing. I couldn't even get hold of any paper to write a letter. Then it occurred to me that you were only a bus ride away.

ANNA: Thank God you've escaped.

MARY: I haven't escaped. I don't know why you have to be so dramatic all the time. (*She begins to get more agitated.*) Mind you, you always had to be different, didn't you? I don't know what else I could have expected. You always were odd. Everybody else marries a man, but not you. It looks as though I've got to resign myself to being the only mother in Acacia Avenue with three sons and four daughters-in-law.

ANNA: Mum, we are not married.

MARY: And why not, that's what I'd like to know. I wouldn't put it past you.

JULIE (*lightly*): I wouldn't have her, she can't iron a shirt to save her life.

MARY: I can quite believe it, Julie. I tried, oh yes, but Madam didn't want to know. I'm surprised she's not entirely defunct on the domestic front.

ANNA (*hurt*): Mum.

MARY: I wouldn't put anything past you. I'm still waiting to find out what was wrong with Kevin.

ANNA: Mum don't . . .

MARY: He was such a nice boy.

JULIE: Kevin?!

ANNA: He was training to be butcher when I was doing my eleven-plus.

MARY: And he worked really hard at it as well. He's his own boss now, you know. (*To* ANNA:) If she'd played her cards right she could have been living over the Dewhurst shop in Camden by now.

ANNA: Am I ever going to win?

Pause.

MARY (*deep breath, then quietly*): Oh dear, I'm sorry, it's lovely to see you. Both of you. The last thing I meant to do was go ranting on. For ages now I've not felt quite right, must be the change of life, but I can't keep blaming that for everything. I became aware that something was definitely wrong when I started to beat the tank.

ANNA (*mouths at* JULIE): Beat the tank?

JULIE (*shrugs and mouths back*): A Potter's Bar expression for masturbation?

MARY: But now I've had the luxury of a whole week to myself and I've come to the conclusion that I don't really mind about it . . . umm, you. You two. Both of you. You know.

ANNA. I'm very pleased. Thanks.

MARY: To tell you the truth, in many ways it comes as a big relief.

ANNA: That's great.

MARY: From the day you were born I've dreaded the speech your father would make at your wedding.

ANNA: Now, in all honesty, I can't say that was one of my reasons.

MARY: I know, I know, I've come to the conclusion that I've worried about a lot of silly things. All my life I've dreaded being thought of as abnormal, while I've based my ideas of normality on David.

ANNA (*ruefully*): Fancy thinking Dad was normal.

MARY: Quite. Mind, you should meet the vicar. He's even more normal.

ANNA: So, you're going to leave him.

MARY: No.

JULIE: Er, I think I'll go and fix dinner. You will stay?

MARY: That's very kind, but I really haven't got time. I'll have to be back at two. David — that's my husband, Anna's father — is picking me up then.

JULIE: Won't they wonder where you've gone?

MARY: They'll wonder all right, but the irony of it is that they won't be able to say anything.

ANNA: How morbid.

MARY: I found it all rather intriguing. Agatha Christie fashion. I kept expecting to find a body in the linen cupboard, but no such luck. Although somebody had torn the last page of Revelation out of the Bible by my bedside.

JULIE: On that optimistic note I'll put the potatoes on.

JULIE *goes out.*

MARY: How nice, you can both make lunch.

ANNA: See, having one daughter-in-law too many could be advantageous.

MARY: Don't push me. Mind, it must be lovely not to have the whole day centred around mealtimes. You know, a lot of things you've said often to me have had a chance to sink in this week and I've made up my mind that when I get home things are going to be done on my terms. (*Pause.*) There, what do you think of that?

ANNA: I don't want to appear to be pouring cold water . . .

MARY: Then don't. I thought you would be pleased.

ANNA: Oh, I am. It's just that you might find it harder than you think. I mean, good intentions are one thing, but trying to put them into practice with Dad . . .

MARY: It's not as though he's a monster, now is it? (*Slight pause.*) Of course, he'll see reason.

ANNA: But . . .

MARY: He's a very reasonable man. He is. Your father is a very reasonable man. Believe it or not he is reasonable. Not quite reason itself, I grant you that, but . . .

ANNA: The words clash.

MARY: Pardon?

ANNA: 'Reasonable' and 'man'. You can't have them together in the same sentence.

MARY: I hope that's not a sample of what gets taught in the classroom today, that half of the population is unreasonable.

ANNA: No.

MARY: I suppose that if it was up to you, the male half of the human race would be cut up for dog food.

ANNA: Don't be daft.

MARY: Sorry. Look, I don't think what you're doing is wrong. I don't know what's right or wrong, but it can't be right for everyone. How can it be? Where would we all be then?

ANNA: Look, I'm not putting it very well. If any change is . . .

MARY: Change? Change? You can't change the weather. Some things you can't change.

ANNA: You just said that you were going to change things at home.

MARY: Quite, but it's one thing claiming to try and change nature, I'm only going to reorganise my kitchen, for goodness' sake.

ANNA: But you're not going to change Dad.

MARY: I don't know why you have to keep putting him down all the time.

ANNA: Because you've wasted the last thirty years of your life wading through the valley of the shadow of marriage.

MARY (kindly): Really, dear, there's no need to take that tone. Goodness me, you make it sound like a living death. You might think that they've been wasted, but let me remind you that you are a direct product of them. I don't think you realise what you're saying half of the time.

ANNA (snaps): That's right, I'm mad.

MARY: I'm sorry.

ANNA: No, it's me. It's just that Dad's so set in his ways — still, that's not for me to say. You know him better than I do.

MARY: At least we're agreed on that. (MARY gets up.) Well, I'd better be . . .

ANNA: I was so worried about you.

MARY: It's me that's supposed to worry about you. It's been lovely to see you. (She turns to go, then says as an afterthought.) I've often wondered,

if anything happened to me, would you ever consider going home to look after them?

ANNA: Let's not end on a sour note.

MARY: Good, I'm very glad of that.

JULIE enters.

JULIE (hands MARY an enormous book entitled What Lesbians do in Bed): I thought you might like this.

MARY: Has it got pictures?

JULIE: 'Fraid not. It's only the theory.

MARY: It's very kind of you, but it's a bit hard to hide behind the spice rack.

JULIE: Oh, not to worry. (She hands MARY a postcard.) I've precised down a few notes.

MARY: Thanks Julie.

ANNA: Good luck.

MARY: Thanks. Bye love.

MARY goes out.

JULIE: Better?

ANNA: I don't know.

JULIE: She didn't seem very vague to me.

ANNA: Bloody hell.

JULIE: Shall I run a hot bath?

ANNA: I hope she's all right.

JULIE: Here, do you want to come with me this evening?

ANNA: Where?

JULIE: I'm meeting Susan, remember? Oh, I don't know, perhaps I better see her on my own, she might be in trouble.

ANNA: Do you mean 'in trouble' trouble or in trouble, trouble in general?

JULIE (sarcastic): I really wish I was as well read as you and then I might be able to express myself with such articulate coherence. (Slight pause.) I didn't particularly mean pregnant but anyway, if she needs to, she could come here.

ANNA: What, come here to live?

JULIE: Yes, it would be a great idea, me and her can . . .

ANNA: Look, why would she want to live here?

JULIE: You saying she can't?

ANNA: No, well, yes.

JULIE: What, why not? Don't tell me, let me guess. You read it in a book. The law according to Sheila Rowbotham. 'Thou shalt not take thy lover's half-sister into your flat.'

ANNA: Our flat.

JULIE: Well then. She'd really enjoy it and the two of us could step up Operation 'Bugger the Open University'.

ANNA: While muggins here goes to work.

JULIE: I can't help your self-righteous fetish for always having to be in the minority.

ANNA (*exasperated*): Oh, I give up.

She slams an exercise book on the table and goes out.

JULIE (*shrugs*): Just a joke.

Blackout.

Scene Eight

SUSAN *sits in the pub, an orange juice in front of her. She is nervous, intensely absorbed in the pattern of her skirt. A* YOUNG MAN *stands at the bar. Presently he comes over to her.*

YOUNG MAN: Quiet in here tonight innit? I don't think I've seen yer in here before. (*He finishes his drink.*) I was jus' about ter git meself another drink, can I git you one?

SUSAN *shakes her head but doesn't look up.*

Not very talkative are yer? I was wondering like, I know this great disco up the road and like it . . .

JULIE *bursts in.*

JULIE (*oblivious of man*): Hello, sorry I'm late.

SUSAN (*looking up relieved*): That's okay.

YOUNG MAN: You two on yer own? I was just explaining ter yer mate, if yer wanted ter come ter this disco . . . it wouldn't cost yer anything on account of . . .

JULIE (*turns to him*): Fuck off.

YOUNG MAN: Like I know the bloke on the door, don't I?

JULIE: Bloody well piss off.

YOUNG MAN (*moving closer*): What about yer friend? Ain't yer goin 'ter let 'er speak fer 'erself?

JULIE: Make one more move, and I'll slit yer throat.

YOUNG MAN: Okay, okay, love. Point taken. (*To* SUSAN:) A real vicious piece of skirt, her. Yer didn't let on you 'ad a bloody guard.

Pause.

Slags.

He goes out.

JULIE (*sits down*): You haven't been here long? Have you?

SUSAN: Nope.

JULIE: Come on, let's get a drink.

Pause.

JULIE: How's things?

SUSAN: Okay. (*Pause.*) You know, awful.

She starts to cry.

JULIE: Hey, I mean, look, I wouldn't have really slit that bloke's throat, would I? I mean if you'd have wanted ter . . .

SUSAN: Christ, no, not that . . .

An OLD MAN *sits next to them, staring into a half-empty pint glass.*

OLD MAN (*looking up*): Here, you two aren't punks, are you?

SUSAN (*to* OLD MAN): Pardon?

JULIE: Take no notice.

OLD MAN: This used to be a nice pub, till those noisy green-haired punks got in.

SUSAN (*to* JULIE): It's just that I want ter talk ter somebody and you're . . .

OLD MAN: What they need is National Service. We need another war. Wouldn't worry about 'ow many earrings they 'ad then, if they was trying not to get their balls shot off.

JULIE: A man after my own heart.

OLD MAN: I was at Dunkirk, y'know, I've got the VC. We saved thousands of men that day. So frantic to get in the boats, they was paddlin' with rifle butts. I bin' in the trenches too, y'know. My best mate got shot to bits. Lay next to me for a fortnight in a canvas bag.

JULIE: All right, mate, what do you want to drink?

OLD MAN: That's very kind of you. A pint of bitter, please.

JULIE *goes to the bar.*

OLD MAN: Not all that bad, you youngsters. What sort of life you got here, eh? This country's all full of lazy jobless scroungers.

JULIE *returns with a pint and a brandy.*

JULIE: On yer bike, action man.

OLD MAN: Why, ta very much, son.

SUSAN (*hisses to* JULIE): Why d'yer do that? He's a fascist.

JULIE: No, he's just a bloody old fool. They all bloody well are. Don't look like we're going ter be able ter git much talkin' done 'ere. Let's go somewhere, an 'ave something ter eat.

SUSAN: Yeh.

Both go out.

Blackout.

Scene Nine

RENE*'s kitchen. One o'clock in the morning.*
RENE *sits in a chair reading* Woman's Own.
ALF, *purple-faced, is slumped over the table with a currant bun in his mouth.*
SUSAN *enters.*
Silence.

RENE (*looks up. Then flatly*): Your father's choked to death on a scone.

Blackout.

Scene Ten

ANNA *and* JULIE*'s kitchen. Two o'clock in the morning.*
JULIE *enters, slumps in a chair, head in hands.*
Pause.
ANNA *enters wearing a dressing-gown.*

ANNA (*forced*): Hi, did you have a good time?

JULIE (*quietly, aggressively*): Barrel of laughs.

Pause.

ANNA (*sarcastic*): Oh good. It's nice to know that you weren't being raped. (*She explodes.*) Where in fuck's name have you been? The pubs shut hours ago. I've been worried sick. Christ, I thought . . .

JULIE: That I'd run off with the bus conductress on the number ninety-eight.

ANNA: You could have phoned.

JULIE: We went for a meal. (*She sighs.*) Do you ever git the feeling that all happiness is at someone else's expense?

ANNA: What did you do? Eat the waiter?

JULIE (*angry*): You want to know something, you can be such a patronising bleedin' . . . bloody . . .

ANNA: Who's stuck for an expletive which isn't exploitative, then?

JULIE: You bleedin' thick dickhead!

ANNA: Well, where is she?

JULIE: What d'you mean, 'Where is she?' You bleedin' well told me she weren't to stay here.

ANNA: When did that ever stop you? Your idea of democratic reasoning can be likened to the chances of a blind cat running in front of a speeding juggernaut.

JULIE: Oh dear me, we've been trying to read Muggeridge again.

ANNA: But of course, once it got out that you were looking for someone to live with she got killed in the crush.

JULIE (*quieter*): She won't leave her mum in the shit, will she?

Pause.

ANNA (*relieved*): That's settled then.

JULIE: Yeah. Want ter know something, eh? You're positively repulsive when you're smug.

The phone rings. Both exchange puzzled glances.

JULIE *picks up the receiver.*

JULIE: 'Lo. Christ, hello. What's happened? Did the old git try and lay inter yer when . . . (*Slight pause.*) Well, what? (*Long pause.*) Yes, love. Right, see yer. Ta taa. Oh, was it a scone or a scon? (*Pause.*)

She replaces the receiver. To ANNA:

My father's dead.

ANNA (*amazed*): God Almighty.

JULIE (*flatly*): No, my father, Alf.

ANNA: How? I mean . . .

JULIE: Drunken sod. Choked to death.

ANNA: Hell . . . what do you feel?

JULIE (*thinks*): Relieved . . . glad.

ANNA: But, Ju, he's dead. I mean it wasn't all his fault.

JULIE (*lightly*): Look love, don't try and spring your ideological unsound criticism crap on me.

ANNA: But . . .

JULIE (*quietly, angry*): You can theorise about anything else you fucking want but don't ever say that to me, not until you've been smashed from one side of the fucking room to the other.

ANNA: Sorry.

Pause.

JULIE: Does that mean Susan can . . .

ANNA: But why should she want to, now?

JULIE: Oh, fuck off!

She goes out.

ANNA: Ju?

Blackout.

Scene Eleven

Monday morning. MARY's *kitchen.*
MARY *is mopping the floor.*
Presently DAVID *enters, fully dressed with the exception of his trousers.*

MARY (*softly singing*):
'Glorious things of thee are spoken,
Zion, City of our God,
Heaven and earth . . .'

DAVID: Good morning, dear. It's so nice to have you back and in such good spirits. A change is as good as a rest. Now you haven't forgotten that Dr Hutchinson, although he may prefer you to call him Marshall — no side to these professionals — is due in a few minutes?

MARY (*pleasantly*): No, dear.

DAVID: I know you're fine, but it's just a check-up, a safety valve. And he's a very useful person to know. I must say that we've all been at sixes and sevens in your absence. Simon tried to iron a shirt but soon found that he had bitten off more than he could chew, ha ha.

MARY (*kindly*): Did he, dear?

DAVID: Still, Mrs Roberts has been a tower of strength, an absolute gem. But it appears that the same old problem has returned, namely that my suit trousers are missing. (*Pause.*) I wonder if you could shed any light on the problem?

MARY mops and sings with an edge of venom.

I can hardly greet a psychiatrist in my underpants, now can I dear?

MARY (*genially*): They're in the garden.

DAVID (*crosses to window*): What, may I presume to ask, are they doing out there? Mary, I can not believe my eyes. My trousers are on the lawn, with a garden roller on top of them.

MARY: Getting a damp press.

DAVID (*anxious not to aggravate her 'problem'*): Curiouser and curiouser.

MARY: Saves pounds on dry cleaning.

DAVID: Would you please bring them in from the garden and I'll be prepared to turn a blind eye.

MARY: David, you are about to hear something which has never been uttered in this kitchen before.

DAVID: Which happens to be what?

MARY (*firmly*): Do — it — yourself.

DAVID (*becoming impatient*): Just how much longer are you going to keep this 'dog in the manger' facade up, eh? Marshall's visit hasn't come a moment too soon. Let me assure you that immediate steps will have to be taken to get you cured. That will knock this stuff and nonsense out of your

sails. (*Pause.*) Mary, I can't go out into the garden in my underwear. Please.

MARY (*sighs*): Don't go away.

She goes out.

DAVID (*mutters*): Why couldn't you take a leaf out of Daphne's books? She's always so sophisticated.

MARY enters with the trousers.

The doorbell rings.

DAVID (*hastily putting on his trousers*): That'll be him now.

DAVID goes out to open the front door and enters with MARSHALL HUTCHINSON.

DAVID: Hello, Dr Hutchinson.

MARSHALL: Hello, David. Do call me Marshall.

DAVID: Do come in.

DAVID (*squirming slightly in his very damp trousers*): Marshall, this is Mary. Mary, this is Dr Hutchinson.

MARSHALL: Good morning, Mrs Johnson.

MARY (*pleasantly*): Good morning, Doctor.

MARSHALL: Do call me Marshall.

DAVID: Nice to see you again, Marshall. How is Mrs Hutchinson?

MARSHALL: She's fairly well, I think. Thank you, David.

DAVID: Well, I'm sorry, but I'm afraid that I really must be off, I'm late for work already. I'm sure you two don't need me anyway, but of course you have the number if you do need to be in touch.

MARSHALL: Right, perhaps I'll do that, and don't forget what we talked about.

DAVID: Yes, right. Fine. (*He kisses MARY, who seems startled by this.*) Bye dear. Goodbye, Marshall.

DAVID *goes out.*

MARY (*calmly*): Please, do sit down.

MARSHALL (*sits at the table*): Thank you.

MARY: Would you like a coffee?

MARSHALL: That would be very nice, thank you.

MARY (*makes coffee, gives cup to MARSHALL, and continued to tidy kitchen*): Sugar?

MARSHALL: No thanks.

MARY: I suppose you'd have that thick brown sugar that tastes like sand.

MARSHALL: No, I've never had sugar.

MARY: Oh good, as long as you're not one of those brown rice and yoga fanatics.

MARSHALL: Do I look like a brown rice and yoga fanatic?

MARY (*still wiping cups, etc.*): No, you look like a bored middle-aged man.

MARSHALL: Would you consider yourself fastidious, fanatical about cleanliness?

MARY: No, I'm sexually frustrated.

Pause.

MARSHALL: And why do you think that is?

MARY: Because I'm married to an emotional eunuch. (*Pause.*) No one ever taught me about sex. I had to learn the hard way.

MARSHALL: Which way was that?

MARY: A lifetime of misery.

MARSHALL: Quite. Look, Mrs Johnson, I am here to try to help you.

MARY: In that case you could have a go at cleaning my cooker.

MARSHALL: I really don't think that would get us very far or solve anything much.

He takes a fountain pen out of his breast pocket, and flicks some ink

on to *a piece of paper, which he folds in half and presents to* MARY.

Now, Mary, what does that represent to you?

MARY (*still wiping round the table, etc.*): A piece of paper with an ink blot on it, folded in half. I hope you haven't come here to flick ink all over my kitchen.

MARSHALL (*sighs*): Do you think you transmitted your disgust of sex to your daughter?

MARY: I never told her anything about it except to screech in a state of semi-hysteria that it was a very beautiful thing in marriage.

MARSHALL: Do you concede that this has undoubtedly been responsible for her immature, perverted and inadequate sexual behaviour in adult life?

MARY: I'm sorry, I don't know about her private affairs. Certainly she never told me of . . .

MARSHALL: You were not aware that she was living with another person of the same sex?

MARY: Oh yes. She's in love with a woman named Julie, oh yes.

MARSHALL: You don't feel that her so-called choice of bed partner has anything to do with your non-communication in her formative years?

MARY: Well, she was breast-fed.

MARSHALL: Mrs Johnson, are you aware of the nature of a sexual relationship between two women, of the insufficiency of human response?

MARY: No.

MARSHALL: Well, a lot of research has been carried out on the subject of female homosexuality, by very learned men. And if you want I'll précis down some of the relevant facts for you.

MARY: Please do. I'm very interested.

MARSHALL: Really, it's a dead loss, and very frustrating too.

MARY: Is that so?

MARSHALL: Yes, these people can only rarely achieve any degree of satisfaction, unless one of the two partners has unusually well-defined physical attributes. For example, occasionally a woman may have an unusually large clitoris, maybe two or even more inches in length.

MARSHALL *holds up his finger and thumb to show the size.*

Now then, if the woman concerned happens to be a lesbian and her partner spreads her legs as wide as she can, well, they may just be able to attain some degree of penetration. Of course, this type of woman is hardly the average, and the normally endowed woman may turn to the dildoe, which in reality is no more than a sponge, rubber or plastic penis.

MARY: But I . . .

MARSHALL: Please let me finish. You must understand that this forever will be the curse of the homosexual, no matter how their tastes are developed, or the success rate they may claim — basically they all end up involved in some parody of normal heterosexual intercourse. The ancient Far East is a common place to look for solutions to problems of this nature, and true to form there is a Japanese device, known as a harigata. Basically a dildoe as I have already described, but designed to be the two-headed member of the family, one head per vagina. Once inserted the partners go through the motions of heterosexual intercourse. I always end up asking myself at this point why they don't just snip it in half, both go home and enjoy themselves at their own leisure.

MARY: Are you sure about this? They seemed so happy to me?

MARSHALL: True happiness depends on a lasting relationship, an option usually denied to homosexuals. Relationships between women do tend to last longer than they do for men — possibly this stems from the male's obsession with anal activities — but they are still full of unhappiness. But male or female, their eventual problem is common to both sexes. They are all looking for satisfaction where there can be no lasting satisfaction. They are all looking for love in a world where there can be no love.

MARY (*very softly*): I think he's talking shit.

MARSHALL: Pardon?

MARY: I think you are talking shit.

MARSHALL (*pause*): Were you aware that you wanted to cannibalise your son's penis?

MARY: I beg your pardon?

MARSHALL: Your husband told me that when your youngest son — Paul, is that right?

MARY: That's right.

MARSHALL: When he quite innocently asked, 'How long's dinner?', you snapped back, 'Four inches, it's a sausage.' Were you aware that you wanted to undermine his sexuality and render him impotent by alluding to the fact that his penis was four inches long and edible?

MARY: I don't know quite how to say this, but I think perhaps you should see a doctor.

MARSHALL: Now that we've got that into the open, it still leaves us with the question of why I'm here and, more to the point, why you are here.

MARY (*firmly*): I am not . . .

MARSHALL: Metaphysically, I'm afraid, the evidence is indisputable.

MARY: I am not mental.

MARSHALL: That's a very old-fashioned word that we no longer like to use these days. Instead we have a less crude, more specifically defined vocabulary of terminology.

MARY: In that case, I'm not psychopathic, hysteric, neurotic, psychotic, paranoic, schizophrenic, manic depressive, hypochondriac, a raving lunatic or a screwball.

MARSHALL: Quite, but we prefer to think of it as an illness. Just as the body can fall sick for no apparent reason so can the mind.

MARY (*louder*): I am not mental.

MARSHALL: Mrs Johnson, I'm afraid . . .

MARY (*screams*): I AM NOT MENTAL.

MARSHALL (*shouts*): YES YOU FUCKING WELL ARE! (*Slight pause.*) Oops, sorry . . . overworked . . . (*Gently.*) Look, why else would I be here? And look at these letters your husband gave me.

He takes some letters from his pockets and starts to read one:

'Dear God, if I have three grown sons, how can it be that I cannot bear to see my husband undressed? Penis running dry. I'm afraid I can't go on.'

MARY (*puzzled, looks at the letter he holds out to her*): No, my 'pen is running dry' i.e. it contains no ink. Therefore . . . I couldn't write anything else after that . . . You seem to be penis-mad. I haven't given the things a second thought in years.

MARSHALL: Do you think that is the evidence of a sane woman?

MARY: How would you know?

MARSHALL: We are supposed to be trained in these matters.

MARY: In being a woman? Impossible. All you're trained in is a load of men's mumbo jumbo garbage. Oh yes, by your values I'm nuts, but by my

values I was — but I am no longer. I've wasted my life in a bitter compromise. I've bitten my lip and said nothing when inside I've been screaming. And when I've practically wanted to wring his neck I've said 'Yes, dear' or 'Whatever you think, dear'. Yes, you win. I was no longer alive, and now I am insane. It's great to feel things, it's just great to be mental. Take any prize you want. Now bum off.

MARSHALL: Let me tell you, it's you with the anal fixation, not me.

Good day.

MARY: Goodbye.

MARSHALL *goes out.*

MARY (*starts to write*): Dearest Anna . . .

Lights fade on MARY.

Lights up on ANNA, *reading a letter she has just finished writing.*

ANNA: Dear Mum, I am writing to tell you how much strength I have gained from our conversation on Sunday, and how much your supportive feelings have meant to me. I think you will probably find things harder than you exected this week, and hopefully I will drop in next Sunday when the old bastard (*She crosses this out.*) when Dad is at church. Take care of yourself, much love Anna.

Lights fade down on ANNA *and fade back up on* MARY, *still writing.*

MARY: . . . and so, dearest Anna . . .

PAUL *enters.*

PAUL: Wotcher, Ma.

MARY: Wotcher, you little grass.

PAUL: Ma?

MARY: Grassing me up about my one and only joke.

PAUL: The 'Four inches, it's a sausage' one?

MARY: What else? You're always so full

of what a humourless cow I am. What other joke could I possibly mean?

PAUL: Gawd, do you have to go on so much?

MARY: What are you doing home this time of day anyway?

PAUL: Sick. Said I was sick.

MARY: Which roughly translated means you've got a bird lined up.

PAUL: Got it in one. But I'm going to watch *Crown Court* first, Okay?

MARY (*gently*): Do you care about me, Paul?

PAUL: Course I do. Bleedin' hell, last week it was bedlam. Blimey, if I didn't care about you would I still be living here? Any chance of something to eat?

MARY: What would you like to eat?

PAUL: We got any toast?

MARY: We've got bread and a toaster. I'm sure it's a simple enough equation for someone with an HND in mechanical engineering.

PAUL: Can't yer give it a bleeding rest?

MARY: Why do you have to talk to me like that?

PAUL: Because I want to, right? Why do you talk like you do?

MARY: Like what?

PAUL: That pathetic simpering.

MARY: I'm sorry.

PAUL: You really get on my nerves. I'll be in my room if you deign to change your mind about the toast.

PAUL *goes out.*

DAVID *enters.*

DAVID: Hello, dear, I came as quickly as I could.

MARY: Why, what's happened?

DAVID: Marshall rang me, he says you definitely qualify for a bed. Can you imagine, a National Health bed? I just popped home to tell you that you can be admitted this evening. It's all right, I'll take you, of course.

MARY: But David . . .

DAVID: Now, Mary, it must be a voluntary admission, for your own good. Once it becomes a Mental Health Section it becomes legally binding. Now I really have to be getting back to the office.

MARY: But David . . .

DAVID: Don't worry about a thing, we'll manage, I'll pick you up. Bye, dear, see you later.

DAVID *goes out.*

MARY: And so, dearest Anna . . .

Long pause while she writes first paragraph, then:

MARY: . . . and so I ask you nothing except for one thing — is that what they call a double bind? — please don't confront the boys or your father over this, but keep quiet. Don't waste any time trying to live up to what you thought my expectations of you were — you have already fulfilled them. I couldn't have loved you more if I'd understood you less, Mum.

She puts ANNA's *letter in an envelope, which she seals and addresses.*

MARY (*writing new letter*): Dear David, your dinner and my head are in the oven.

She crosses to the cooker, finds a comfortable position, turns on the gas and puts her head in the oven.

Fade. Blackout.

Scene Twelve

RENE. *Monologue.*

RENE: It's bin ages since I seen a show. I don't rightly see the point of 'em myself. With my life I 'aven't 'ad no room for dramatic art — know what I mean? What I call good entertainment is the royal wedding — no, it might surprise you to know that I don't love 'em and, to be honest with you, I do feel if we've paid for it and let's face it, we have — they could have all have made the effort to look nice. For my money the Queen looked a frump, well, didn't she? Mind, I say that but I wouldn't 'ave her job fer the world but if the truth be known when Mountbatten copped his lot I didn't feel anything. If you want to know something, I almost breathed a sigh of relief when I heard the Pope had bin shot. Would you trust a man who vowed never to have sex? I don't mean to be funny but if God hadn't meant us to do it, he'd 'ave put pollen on our plates, wouldn't he? Don't get me wrong, I'm not saying I wished him dead but when I saw him sitting up in hospital I felt me hopes had been dashed. I know it's wrong. It was wrong. It's just like with Alf passing on so suddenly I seem to have death on the brain. Police come round, didn't they, insinuating that it was mighty peculiar that the body was cold before the doctor was called but even they have to accept the coroner's verdict of death by misadventure, not before they'd turned the whole place upside down, I might add.

And terday, y'know, I woke up and I felt different — everything seemed to have changed. Susan and me had breakfast together and we didn't have to whisper or try frantically to hush the Rice Krispies up. I was an old nag I was, I used to rabbit on and on and yesterday evening, coming home from the bus stop on me own I started to get that nervy feeling again but I ain't never bin beaten up or raped ourside me own home. For twenty-four hours a day I lived with that fear . . . Oh Gawd, don't start me off. When Susan was in hospital she met this woman who used to go on all the time you know, she was a bit like that Julie nutter except for — don't try and tell me — career or family or both, it don't seem to make no difference — still moaning I said ter her, I said, that's the trouble with us, we don't seem ter know what we want. We 'ad this long conversation, really nice girl she was, but I can't fathom some of them words and I don't want nothing what I can't understand. But I do understand one thing now. Like even if in the future I met a nice respectable man and even if I was to marry him — he nor any man wouldn't mean that much in comparison to what my daughter means to me.

Scene Thirteen

A hospital room.
MARY *in bed, semi-conscious.*
Presently THREE WOMEN *enter.*

MARY (*mumbles*): What? Where? Oh, er. What's . . .

OLD WOMAN: It's all right dear, you're perfectly okay. You're safe.

MARY: How? How did I get here? What happened? Who are you?

OLD WOMAN: Gently now. Try and give yourself room to think.

MARY: Oh, no. I feel so ashamed. It must be a month since I cleaned my cooker. Smell my hair.

OLD WOMAN: Mmm. Roast beef. Hadn't you been converted to North Sea Gas. It's not poisonous, so I am told.

MARY: No, the cooker was too old.

She smiles.

Oh dear, fancy talking about the state of my cooker the minute I come round from . . . well.

OLD WOMAN: I don't worry. I'm usually greeted with, 'How many calories are there in a hundred valium?'

MARY (*to herself*): Funny matron.

OLD WOMAN (*gently*): I am here to tell you that I love you and have done so all your life. I am ahead of myself. Introductions first. I am the deity.

MARY (*confused, to* TALL WOMAN): I suppose she means the day-ity shift as opposed to the night-y.

OLD WOMAN (*gesturing to* TALL WOMAN): This is the Holy Hostess with the mostest and this (*She gestures to* YOUNG WOMAN.) is my daughter who bled in a shed for you — and for many.

Silence.

MARY (*panics*): Now hold on a minute, what sort of hospital is this? It's a loony bin, isn't it? He's had me committed to the bin.

She is frightened.

OLD WOMAN (*takes hold of* MARY's *hand*): No, Mary, you're in paradise.

MARY (*shouts*): Christ alive. I'm dead!

YOUNG WOMAN (*smiles*): No need to call up false images.

MARY: But I mean, I never got the feeling that God approved of me.

OLD WOMAN (*shrugs*): That's just as well. He doesn't exist.

MARY: But I, oh . . .

OLD WOMAN (*kindly*): You are here, like other women, because your life was at best monotonous, and at worst unbearably painful. But you have the choice to go back to where you left off.

MARY: Go back?

OLD WOMAN: Yes. To that awful existence you call life. I can assure you that you won't have to do anything you don't want to.

MARY: Excuse me, but what happens to men? In the Bible it says . . .

TALL WOMAN (*shrieks*): That libellous load of crap!

OLD WOMAN: That is a myth created by men in their fear. Men don't have eternal life. How could they? They have no souls. You must have noticed. They're all two-dimensional.

YOUNG WOMAN: Just bloody bores . . . excuse my menstrual jargon.

MARY: So you can beam me back to Earth? Like on *Star Trek*?

TALL WOMAN: That libellous load of crap.

OLD WOMAN (*smiles*): What sort of hostess are you? Honestly, you'd think she'd learnt only one colloquial expression from the world of man. (*All three shudder.*) Mary, you are in a twilight zone. The choice is yours.

MARY: But my daughter . . .

OLD WOMAN: Remember, I am with you. If you go back I will do all I can to help you stand against that war-ridden shit heap men call earth.

MARY: Who'd have thought the deity would say shit?

Slight pause.

I must go back.

OLD WOMAN: As you wish.

MARY: At least until she's happily married.

Thunder roars, lightning flashes.

What am I saying?

TALL WOMAN: Take it from me, Mary. She's found something better than that load of crap.

OLD WOMAN: There you go again.

TALL WOMAN: Well you said shit.

MARY: If I decide to go back, can you give me the power to put the fear of God — I beg your pardon — into those men.

OLD WOMAN (*shakes her head and smiles*): I'm sorry, Mary, but we simply know no fear.

MARY: In that case . . .

I'm home.

Immediate blackout.

From the complete darkness we hear ROGER *in his official capacity.*

ROGER: Forasmuch as it hath pleased Almighty God of his great mercy to take unto himself the soul of our dear sister here departed: we therefore commit her body to the ground, earth to earth, ashes to ashes, dust to dust;

Lights up on MARY's *kitchen.*

DAPHNE *is at the table making cucumber sandwiches. There is a tray of full sherry glasses on the table.*

ROGER *and* DAVID *are drinking tea.*

DAVID: I really can't thank you enough. It was a very moving service.

ROGER: That's quite all right, old boy. It was the very least I could do in the circumstances.

DAVID: I only have ten years left before I retire.

ROGER: Rotten. Rotten bad luck.

DAPHNE (*screams*): Rotten bad luck. (*She checks herself quietly.*) Roger, she reached despair, she killed herself.

DAVID: I'll thank you to keep a civil tongue in your head. Mary was always very careless about leaving the oven door open. It is my opinion that she tripped up and fell asleep before she had time to get up.

ROGER (*nods*): All part of God's rich plan.

DAPHNE: God has a wondrous philosophy, you know what it is, eh?

ROGER: Come along, Daphners, old girl.

DAPHNE: Do you want to know what it is, eh, David? Yes, of course you do. It is this. No sooner does one door shut than the whole fucking house falls in.

ROGER (*pats* DAVID *on the back*): Rest assured we're all in God's hands.

DAPHNE (*screams, for she has now lost her head*): What's he doing then? Having a jolly good wank with us all?

DAPHNE *goes out.*

ROGER: I'm going to have to get on to Marshall over this. Do you mind if I use the phone?

DAVID: Please do. She is obviously very sick.

ROGER: Her guilt has turned inwards and consumed her. Shan't be a mo.

Both go out.

Blackout.

ANNA *and* JULIE *enter.*

ANNA *wears a black skirt and tee-shirt.* JULIE *has probably conformed to a pair of black dungarees.*

ANNA (*looks round kitchen picking up things and putting them down*): What didn't I do?

JULIE: I don't know.

ANNA: Was I too arrogant? Did I give her enough room to say what she wanted?

JULIE: I don't know.

ANNA (*smiles*): And I thought you knew everything. C'mon, let's go home.

Both hug each other to be interrupted by DAPHNE – *kicking the furniture as she re-enters.*

DAPHNE: Bastards. Gits. I'm going to kill them, I am. I'm going to strangle them with a cheese wire and I'll not be satisfied until I see their severed heads bobbing up and down in a washing-up bowl.

ANNA (*gently*): Please . . .

DAPHNE: Why did she want to keep quiet, look where it got her. (*Louder.*) Look where it got her. She's dead. For Chrissakes! She's dead.

She pulls two knobs off the cooker and gives them one each.

There, I have metaphorically castrated your mother's murderer, pulled the knobs off the cooker, ha ha!

JULIE: Daphne? Please.

DAPHNE: I'm not mad. For Christ's sake. I'm angry. (*She smiles.*) Don't worry. I'll sabotage tonight's salad — rinse the lettuce in Dettol.

Blackout.

Scene Fourteen

MARY*'s kitchen.*
    ROGER *and* DAVID *begin to set out the game of Monopoly.*

DAVID: Shall we play to the nearest ten pounds?

ROGER: That's not a bad idea. I'll have to be going at three if I'm to get to see Daphne.

DAVID: How is she these days?

MARY (*voice off, softly*): David . . .

    DAVID *is mildly disconcerted as though he has heard something far away.*

ROGER: They've done wonders since she first went in. When I managed to speak to the top bod he said that in all his years of psychiatric care he'd never seen anyone in such mental anguish.

DAVID: Despite the fanatical support for Church unity one can't help feeling that those Christian Scientists are definitely barking up the wrong tree. If the Lord hadn't intended Largactil to be invented he wouldn't have given men such marvellous minds.

MARY (*voice off*): But David . . .

    DAVID *seems slightly irritated but dismisses it.*

ROGER: True. Mind, Monopoly isn't the same without her.

DAVID: No. In fact it's never been the same since I lost my tank.

ROGER: Here, use the gun. The curate in my last parish told me that when Runcie was a canon he always used to play with the gun.

MARY (*off*): You know where you can poke the gun.

    Tank drops from height to the table.

ROGER: Talk of the devil. Here it is.

DAVID: Mrs Roberts has been stupendous. I can't imagine what we'd have done without her.

MARY (*off*): Mother Almighty, what, tell me, is the point?

    Blackout.

THE DEVIL'S GATEWAY

The Devil's Gateway was first presented at the Royal Court Theatre Upstairs, London, on 24 August 1983 with the following cast:

BETTY	Pam Ferris
IVY	Rita Triesman
CAROL ⎫ FIONA ⎭	Lizzie Queen
ENID	Susan Porrett
LINDA	Chrissie Cotterill
JIM ⎫ MR GARDNER SOCIAL SECURITY OFFICER ⎬ POLICEMAN ⎭	Roger Frost

Directed by Annie Castledine
Designed by Annie Smart
Lighting designed by Val Claus

Scene One

Second-floor flat in Bethnal Green.
BETTY'*s living-room which incorporates*
kitchen area. Although the furniture is
old everything is spotlessly clean. The
room is brightened by several 'cheap'
ornaments, i.e. a brandy glass with a
china cat up the side, A bright orange
luminous ashtray on a stand.
　　JIM *and* CAROL *are watching*
Nationwide, *having finished their meal,*
IVY *is still eating hers.* BETTY *is*
washing-up.

BETTY: Sometimes I feel like a
　　washing-up machine on legs. I don't
　　know why we don't get paper plates.
　　(*Nobody is listening.*) Oh Betty, talk
　　to yourself then.

JIM: Bet, Bet, come on, Lady Diana's
　　on next.

CAROL: You already told us, Dad.

JIM: I know but you know what she's
　　like, faffing about.

BETTY: Who's she? Thank you very
　　much.

JIM: And if you miss it, who'll get the
　　blame? Me, that's who. Come and sit
　　down Bet or you'll miss it.

BETTY: Keep your hair on. (*She dries*
　　her hands and crosses to the telly.)
　　I can't see her.

JIM: That's because they're still talking
　　to that bunch of headcases. I told you,
　　she's on after this.

CAROL: Is Joe-Joe all right, Mum?

JIM: Stop calling him that cissy name,
　　Carol. He's named after his grandad,
　　Big Jim and Little Jim.

BETTY (*crosses to the window and looks*
　　out): They seem to be playing happily.
　　(*Pause.*) Whoops.

CAROL: What's happened? (*She gets*
　　up.)

BETTY: Don't worry, a little
　　misunderstanding about whose trike it
　　was but Joe-Joe has left them in no
　　confusion.

CAROL: Shall I call him in?

BETTY: No, no, it's all okay now. (*She*
　　comes back to the telly and sits
　　down.)

JIM: Gawd, this is going on a bit. I
　　reckon you've got time to put the
　　kettle on. (BETTY *pretends not to*
　　hear this.) Just look at them, would
　　yer. Mad, mad as hatters. They should
　　be interviewing the blokes that work
　　there.

CAROL: Dad, nuclear power isn't news,
　　it's a fact of life and those women
　　because they're weird make news.
　　Darrel reckons soon it will all be
　　forgotten and we'll have a spate of
　　Alsatian dogs biting children next
　　week.

JIM: Huh, you wait till we get this cable
　　TV. God only knows what sort of
　　Russian infiltration we'll get then.

CAROL: Don't be daft, it's just a silly
　　stunt.

JIM: Just look at it. Look at the state of
　　it. I'm surprised those kids haven't
　　been taken into care.

BETTY: What is it?

IVY: This potato's got lumps in.

BETTY: It can't have, Mum, it's Smash.

IVY: Well, the water couldn't have been
　　hot enough. It's cracking round me
　　dentures.

BETTY: D'you want some more?

IVY: No, ta, look, can I turn over for
　　Crossroads now?

JIM: We haven't seen Lady Diana yet.

IVY: Who wants to see her? Traipsing
　　round another nursery looking very
　　embarrassed.

JIM: With the baby, you daft bat.

IVY: Another mouth to feed.

BETTY: Go on, Mum, turn over.
(BETTY *gets up to make the tea.*)

IVY (*switches channels by using the remote control which is on the arm of her chair*): Ta Betty.

JIM: Turn it down for the adverts – just look at that would yer, Carol? Would you look at that? Modern technology, that is, just point it at the set. No wires, no nothing. Only put one pound fifty on the rental. Can you credit that, one pound fifty for something that brilliant. You should get Darrel to invest in one.

CAROL: He won't have anything on HP or rental. He says (*She tries to recall his exact words.*) It's immediate gratification for people who live from day to day. (*Then:*) It took us a year to save for our telly but it's worth it 'cos it's ours.

BETTY (*from the washing-up bowl*): Oh yeah, madam. For your information this is not like on the knock yer know, 'cos shall I tell you something, if anything goes wrong with our set they come out and replace it the same day. Now, if your big valve goes, that's going to set you back another three hundred quid and that will probably mean you put your brass toilet holders in hock.

CAROL: Gold-plated dolphin toilet-*roll* holders. And anyway, you'll have paid for that set twenty times over before you're finished, Darrel says.

BETTY: Well, you tell Darrel, how comes he's got a whacking great mortgage 'cos you'll have paid fifty times over for that rabbit hutch when you've finished. Tell him to put that up his panatella and smoke it.

JIM: You hoovered in here today, Bet?

BETTY: You know full well I do the hoovering on Wednesdays and Fridays.

JIM: Even so it's looking a bit grubby.

BETTY: Maybe if we all concentrated on getting the food from our plate into our mouths instead of studying what was on the carpet we wouldn't have time to drop it there in the first place.

JIM: Okay, I was only asking.

BETTY: Sorry, it's just if I do it now, it'll be grubby again by Friday.

IVY: Don't do it now. We won't hear *Crossroads*.

CAROL: Nanny, do you think we could turn over to *Star Trek* at a quarter to? It's Joe-Joe's favourite.

IVY: He doesn't seem too bothered to me.

CAROL: Nanny, please.

IVY: Fair enough. (*She shouts in the direction of the window:*) Son, do you want to see *Star Trek*? If you don't speak up, you want *Crossroads*.

CAROL: Nan! He can't hear you.

IVY: Nan nothing. Manners maketh man, Nan, that's what he's trying to say. Really he's as anxious as me to know what happened to Diane and Mr Paul.

CAROL: Darrel says *Crossroads* is bad television.

BETTY: Lucky then that Darrel is a solicitor's clerk and not the Controller of ITV.

CAROL: He is a solicitor, not a clerk.

BETTY: I thought he was doing his columns.

CAROL: His articles.

JIM (*to* BETTY): So what have you bin doing today?

BETTY: Well, I did the bedrooms, took the washing to the launderette.

JIM: Yeah, you spend all week in there, gassing if you ask me.

BETTY: Then I came home. Me and mum 'ad dinner. Then we went shopping. We had to wait half hour for the bus to Stratford and half hour coming back.

JIM (*winks at* CAROL): Is that all? What else did you do?

BETTY: Cooked your bloody tea. I haven't sat down for five minutes.

JIM: I s'pose you and her had your dinner on the bus.

IVY: Go on, tell big mouth what you nearly did today. That'll show him, tiresome bugger.

CAROL: Nanny!

BETTY: Shut up Mum, you're a real stirrer you are. As Enid would say, a real devil's avocado.

JIM: I might have guessed Enid was behind it.

BETTY: I never did nothing. Mum, I could kill you. I never did it.

JIM: Did what? Well, what Betty . . .? I'm waiting.

BETTY: It's nothing to get het up over. I was only thinking mind, that maybe I should go to Carol's old school and ask if they needed a dinner lady, like, to help out.

JIM: Have you gone stark staring crackers, woman?

BETTY: Now Jim, Jim, now Jim, Jim. I was only thinking about it.

JIM: How many times have I told you, Betty? For God's sake, woman, listen once and for all. I am worried every day that the Social Security are going to catch up with me, every day. You don't want to start going out to work and all, otherwise we'll all be in jail and anyway, the money you'd earn would be like a piss in the ocean.

IVY: Shut it, Brian Clough. I can't hear the telly.

CAROL: He's right, Mummy, it wouldn't be fair.

BETTY: Yes, I only thought about it. I didn't do anything.

JIM: And you won't, will ya?

BETTY: No. (*Pause.*) Where on earth is John? This is the third time I've had to throw his tea away this week.

JIM: He can look after hisself, Bet, don't worry. When I was his age perhaps a bit older, I was doing my National Service.

BETTY: Yeah, so is he on a YOP's-flops course.

JIM: Now you're being silly.

BETTY: Say what you like but I wouldn't want him over in the Falklands, thank you very much.

JIM: Nor would I Betty, nor would I, but someone had to go.

BETTY: Why?

JIM: What do you mean, why? Because the people of this country are not going to be pushed around.

IVY: Since when?

JIM: Are you watching *Crossroads* or not?

CAROL. I'll make the tea, Mum. (*She gets up to pour the tea.*)

BETTY: I don't see why they couldn't have played a football match over them.

JIM: You are being totally ridiculous, Betty.

CAROL: It's more complex than that, Mummy.

IVY: For a start, two Argentinians play for Spurs.

BETTY. Huh, load of silly boys' games if you ask me, but then they never grow up, do they, Carol?

CAROL: I hope you're not including Darrel in that? He supports Women's Lib. Won't hear a word against Mrs T. and let's face it, she gave the orders.

BETTY: Well, I never liked her much.

JIM: No one in their right mind does.

BETTY: The only nice thing about her is her hairdo.

JIM: That's right, you stick to something

you know about. You know something, my wife's so outta touch with the world she thought the handbrake in the car was the clutch because you clutched it in your hand. It wasn't until I paid out for a driving instructor and he asked her to put her foot on the clutch that she learnt her lesson.

BETTY: Bloody sprained my ankle trying to stamp on that stick from a sitting position.

CAROL: I've heard all this one hundred times.

IVY: You'll hear it a hundred times more and all. It's a real bone of contention between them.

JIM: Complete waste of money more like.

BETTY: They were your idea.

JIM: Only 'cos you kept moaning.

BETTY: Anyhow, we had to get rid of the car so where's the point in going on about it?

JIM: See this, Carol, and take note not to get like this at her age. Nothing suits her and course to get out of it she reckons men, who let's face it, run the world without fussing about hairdos, are little boys. I ask you.

BETTY: Don't you remember, Jim, when you worked on the print and found out how close this country came to it in that Cuban crisis? You were only little at the time, Carol, and that night we stood over your bed and cried, didn't we, Jim?

JIM: You did, Betty. I had a bad cold if you remember.

BETTY: And we said what sort of world had we brought her into.

CAROL. Better watch out, Dad, or we'll be seeing mum chained to the railings in some windswept corner of the woods.

JIM: Huh, she can't even find her way to the launderette, let alone Newbury bog.

BETTY: What is? What are you talking about?

JIM: Those women on the telly.

BETTY: What? What's he on about?

CAROL: Where've you been? There are a group of women living rough on some common as a protest.

BETTY: What protest? What common?

CAROL: They don't like the idea of nuclear weapons.

BETTY: Oh. (*Pause.*) Does anyone?

CAROL: But it's a bit naive, not to say daft.

BETTY: But why live on a common? Why not sit in the Houses of Parliament?

JIM (*exasperated*): Because the common is where the government is hoping to put the missiles.

BETTY: Oh.

JIM: It's silly because they think they'll stop them. Ha ha ha. Bunch of lunatics.

CAROL: But if misguided people did sit up and take notice then we'd be in a worse mess. Just because we get rid of weapons the Russians won't and we'll have cut our own throats, literally. Darrel says.

BETTY (*innocently*): I don't see why anyone's got to have them.

JIM (*weary*): You silly born bitch. How stupid can you get — know all, know nothing. You'd have us all dancing about with bows and arrows, charging through the bushes, you would. Betty, we are living in a highly civilised age of technology, thank God.

BETTY: Thank God? Well, I wouldn't be thanking God if I was sitting under a table with you lot, four cans of baked beans and a plastic rubbish bag to put the dead bodies in.

JIM: We wouldn't have time, Betty, so don't worry about it.

BETTY (*sarcastic*): Oh that's nice. What a relief, I'll stop worrying then.

CAROL: Actually, Darrel was talking about the possibility of getting a mortgage for a fall-out shelter.

IVY: Oh that's good, we'll all come round on the big day.

CAROL: Well, Nanny, we haven't got a very big garden as you know.

BETTY: What have we got?

IVY: There'll be a riot if the lift's out of order.

CAROL: Anyway, you only get a four-minute warning.

BETTY: Oh, console us. Interesting to see what everyone will do with the last four minutes on earth.

CAROL: Darrel says, ironically it would make a very interesting study of human nature.

JIM: Maybe all those sociologist people could arrange a trial run.

BETTY: And what are you planning to do in those four minutes Lord Jim?

JIM (*considers this*): A bit of hanky panky with my wife.

BETTY: And then what?

CAROL: Mummy!

BETTY: Well, that's only two minutes gone. I tell you, Carol, I just have time to say, 'You've left your socks on again,' and it's all over.

IVY *laughs*.

JIM: What are you laughing at?

IVY: David Hunter forgot his lines.

CAROL: Mummy! Really!

BETTY: What's with this, 'Mummy' malarky bit? You'll be saying 'my husband and I' next. You might have the lifestyle of Princess Margaret but let me remind you, you're not related to royalty.

CAROL: I don't need any reminding, you're so flippin' crude.

BETTY: Crude? Flippin'?? What sort of word is that, can you believe this, Mum, your granddaughter?

IVY (*flatly – still watching the telly*): I told you Bet. I thought it was a miracle her getting up the club. Reminds me of the old song about God Almighty lifting up her nighty.

CAROL: Do you have to be so vulgar, Nanny? Think of Joe-Joe.

IVY: I was.

BETTY (*to* CAROL): Oh and just where do you think you came from?

JIM: Do you mind?! I've just eaten.

BETTY (*to* CAROL): I suppose you think Harrods flew you here in a Tupperware picnic basket with gold-plated shark handles.

CAROL: Frankly, sometimes I'd prefer to think that. Anyway, how many more times, it's gold-plated dolphin toilet-roll holders. I think it's time I was going. Darrel will be home soon and we're going out tonight.

BETTY (*pleased*): Oh Joe-Joe can stay here.

CAROL: It's okay. Thanks, but we've arranged for next door to babysit. Darrel says it's reciprocal. They do it for us and I do it for them.

BETTY: I'm not good enough then?

CAROL: Don't be like that, Mum. Mind you, I'm glad he's playing outside. God alone knows how his vocabulary would be improved if he'd have picked up any of the conversation in here.

BETTY: He's got to know the facts of life, you can't bring him up on a load of rubbish.

CAROL: That's a laugh coming from you. I had to leave home before I discovered Tampax doesn't ruin your married life.

BETTY: They can do if you keep them in.

JIM: Just leave it out will ya?

IVY: Don't you bring your sanitary towel talk in here, madam, not in mixed company. Where are you off tonight, a husband-swapping party?

CAROL: Theatre actually.

IVY (*disappointed*): Oh. (*Then*:) What is it, *No Sex Please We're British*?

CAROL: No, *The Importance of Being Earnest.*

IVY: You'll like that. He was born in a handbag.

CAROL: See you next week then.

BETTY: I'll come and say goodbye to Joe-Joe.

CAROL: Oh Dad, when you see John, would you tell him that Darrel has found that old air rifle if he would like to call round for it.

BETTY: He'll do no such thing. Jim, do you hear me? Jim, I am not having that thing in the flat.

IVY: Certainly not. Before I know where I am, I'll have a jacksee full of lead. I'm a sitting target.

JIM: Bit of luck he'll aim fer yer boat. That'll shut a few gobs round here.

CAROL: Bye Dad, Nanny.

CAROL *and* BETTY *move out of the earshot of* JIM *and* IVY.

BETTY: You and Darrel haven't decided yet on whether or not to go in for another little brother or sister for Joe-Joe?

CAROL: Oh Mum, Darrel was really torn, so he tossed a coin and the Mini Metro came up heads.

BETTY: Huh, as if British Leyland hasn't got enough to answer for. Besides, I don't think much of that as an idea to enforce population control.

CAROL: Anyhow, Joe-Joe's still young and we've got to get on our feet.

BETTY: Can't you arrange for an accident?

CAROL: What on earth for? We can't afford a fully comp. insurance policy.

BETTY: Not to the car —to you. You know . . .

CAROL: No, I couldn't. God, Mum, that's more than my life's worth. Besides, there's something to be said for taking responsibility.

BETTY: For what?

CAROL: For thinking what sort of world you're bringing a child into.

BETTY: Gawd help us, if everyone carried on like that there'd be more dodos running about than humans. (*Pause.*) Take care, love.

CAROL: And you. (*She kisses her.*) See you soon.

CAROL *goes out,* BETTY *returns to the others.*

JIM: What was all that about?

BETTY: Women's talk.

JIM: Oh Gawd, that only means one thing — trouble.

BETTY: D'you think she's okay?

JIM: Yes. She's fine. You always fuss too much.

IVY (*without looking up*): She's okay. It's the bleedin' chinless wonder she married what's a pain in the bum.

JIM: The fact that you don't like him is enough recommendation for me.

BETTY: Do you think she's ashamed of us?

JIM: Look, Betty, she wanted to better herself. You can't blame her for that and she's done all right by him. I for one am proud of that.

BETTY: Umm . . .

JIM: Darrel's an all right bloke as it happens, he is. Think back, Betty, some of the potential son-in-laws we could've got landed wiv, it's a wonder we ain't on our knees thanking God everyday.

BETTY: Well, I wouldn't go that far, Jim.

JIM: Huh, one thing's for sure, if she'd ave married that dead-head Ted she'd ave bin up Pentonville visiting him every other week. (*Pause.*) Come to think , that's where I'll be an all if the Social catch on about me job.

BETTY: Don't say that, Jim. Anyhow they can't send you away for that; there'd be more in than out.

JIM: At one time, Betty, I used to reckon the scrounging sods deserved all they got.

BETTY: I remember.

JIM: Makes you think don't it.

IVY (*sighs*): Can't be all bad then.

Scene Two

FIONA *and* LINDA*'s squat in Hackney.* FIONA *is ironing a dress.* LINDA *enters.*

LINDA: You're early.

FIONA: Yeah, but I've got to go to another bloody boring meeting in a minute.

LINDA (*noticing the dress*): Oh no, not again.

FIONA: 'Fraid so. I won't have time to do it tomorrow morning.

LINDA (*picks up the dress by the sleeve and sniffs the armpit*): Phew, when was the last time you washed it? It could stand up by itself. All you do is throw it in the bottom of the wardrobe and iron it when duty calls.

FIONA: Who cares?

LINDA: I thought the whole point of social workers wearing a dress in court was to create a good impression.

FIONA: Yeah.

LINDA: Can't imagine it going down too well you standing there stinking like a three-week-old meat pie.

FIONA (*laughs*): There are no rules about what you smell like.

LINDA: Just as well there's no law against it. Although there probably will be one day.

FIONA: I bloody hate it. Every time it's such an ordeal.

LINDA: Not half the ordeal it is for the poor bugger in the dock.

FIONA (*agreeing*): Okay, but what difference should it make what I wear? Oh, moan, moan, moan. How was your day?

LINDA: Bag of laughs.

FIONA: You don't stink none too healthy yourself.

LINDA (*sending* FIONA *up*): Being the chief fish fryer at Littlewoods canteen is not without ordeal or responsibilities you know.

FIONA: What responsibilities?

LINDA: Making sure the oil's hot enough. The batter's thick enough and that mad Annie doesn't dice the fish and put them in the trifles.

FIONA: She sounds wonderful.

LINDA: Gets beyond a joke sometimes. Today right, she gets all the dish cloths, dips 'em in batter and they only get sent down as cod. (*They both laugh.*) I don't know why I'm laughing, I nearly got the bleedin' sack over it.

FIONA: Gawd, how did you explain that away?

LINDA: With a lot of difficulty. Still certainly breaks the monotony working with someone with a run amok brain. Lucky she lives in this borough, otherwise you'd be her social worker.

FIONA: Oh, that reminds me, I've got to see a family who live in the same block as your mum.

LINDA: Never was a problem estate until our lot moved in, we set a trend.

FIONA: No real derangements. The son was fast becoming a hardened glue-sniffer till we got him on a YOP's course.

LINDA: You fraud, pushing kids into those.

FIONA (*agreeing*): Umm. (*Then:*) At least it keeps 'em off the streets and I s'pose carpentry is a practical skill.

LINDA: Right. Now he can cement his nostrils together with Plasticwood to his lungs' content.

FIONA: I think they must live on the floor above yours.

LINDA: The mother's name's not Betty?

FIONA: I'm not sure. I think the grandmother's name's Ivy.

LINDA: Gordon Bennett, I went to school with her daughter.

FIONA: Don't be daft, she must be pushing fifty.

LINDA: Not Ivy's, Betty's, Carol.

FIONA: Who?

LINDA: Carol's Mum is Betty. Betty's Mum is Ivy. Carol is Betty's daughter. Betty is . . .

FIONA: Okay, Okay . . . but I don't think the youngest, Carol? right? is living at home.

LINDA: Na, she went through a very unfortunate phase at school and ended up marrying him.

FIONA: Shame. Suburban maisonette job?

LINDA: Worse. Stripped pine Islington job.

FIONA: She'd know your mum then.

LINDA: Doubt it. Betty does.

FIONA: You haven't told her you're living with me?

LINDA: No, I told her I was living with the Olympic women's caber-tossing champion.

FIONA: I mean where I work and that?

LINDA: Don't worry, I said you was the personnel manageress at Littlewoods.

FIONA: Trust you.

LINDA: Well, it pleased her that I had illusions of upward mobility. She worked her way up from knickers you know.

FIONA: Pardon?

LINDA: She started on the knicker counter and worked her way up.

FIONA (*laughs*): Charming. (*She has finished ironing and starts to throw things into a rucksack.*)

LINDA: You should be flattered it's a good job, lot of responsibility. You can determine how long someone can stay in the sick room if they have a period pain.

FIONA: Power.

LINDA: If she likes you, you can get anything up to four hours. If she don't, ten minutes.

FIONA: How long do you get?

LINDA: I keep a bottle of Paracetamol in my locker just in case.

FIONA (*looking up from rucksack*): You sure you can't take tomorrow off?

LINDA: Sorry. No.

FIONA: You don't want to go anyway though, do you?

LINDA: What for?

FIONA: Little thing like an interest in life.

LINDA: Boring. (*Pause.*) The way I see it, there are more important things to get excited about.

FIONA: Nothing will matter in the event of a nuclear war, I'm sure even NATO don't care if sex shops go up.

LINDA: Oh yeah? You try explaining that to the woman who's raped and killed out there tonight. Shame you couldn't stick around, love, and see the war what might or might not have bin.

FIONA: So we sort it all out — then get blown sky high?

LINDA: Oh, and so by some miracle we do stop it. Then we can all go back and not worry about anything ever again. Yip, yip, yippee.

FIONA: Perhaps you start at the worse end of the scale.

LINDA: But anyway, what has it got to do with women? That's what I want ter know?

FIONA: Apart from the fact that we're fifty-two per cent of the population. Besides, it's a way of reaching women.

LINDA: Huh.

FIONA: Huh? HUH nothing. It's a household word.

LINDA: Huh? Huh is a household word?

FIONA: Greenham Common (*She looks at her watch.*) Shit is that the time? I must go.

LINDA: You find me one woman that you see in your job who knows about it . . .

FIONA: And you'll go . . . (*She crosses to the door.*)

LINDA: Who doesn't think they're a bunch of lunatics, then I might go . . .

FIONA: Deal.

LINDA: For a picnic.

FIONA *goes out.* LINDA *finishes ironing the dress.*

Scene Three

ENID *and* BETTY. BETTY *is ironing.*

BETTY: Took the best part of yesterday morning to do all this stuff. I had to lug it up to Cambridge Heath and all.

ENID: What about the one round the corner?

BETTY: You should see the two and eight it's in. Nothing works.
You can feel the tension between putting your money in and waiting for the light to come on.

ENID: Gawd, I couldn't have lugged that lot up there.

BETTY (*not nastily*): Last time you did your washing in public was with a bar of soap and a scrubbing board.

ENID: I've told you often enough you can use my machine.

BETTY: Jim won't hear of it. Anyhow the exercise done me good. I've put on about seven pounds in the last couple of months.

ENID: Well, I didn't like to say nothing but you really should start coming to Weightwatchers again.

BETTY: No thanks, I can't cope with it.

ENID: It does work Betty, it does. You know together we give each other strength.

BETTY: Enid, there are three things I believe you should do in private. Breast-feeding, going to the toilet and weighing yourself.

ENID: Don't be such a paradon of virtue, weighing yourself isn't dirty.

BETTY: No, but it's embarrassing.

ENID: That's what gives you the insensitive though, don't it? Besides going there on Thursday means I'm out when money-grabbing Molly comes round with the poxy catalogue.

BETTY: Here, John told me a joke about that.

ENID: Think about it, Betty, you know you always tell the punchline first.

BETTY: What lies in the grass and goes ding dong?

ENID: A snake with a bell on its prick.

BETTY: No, no, a dead Avon lady.

ENID: Gawd, is that it? My answer was better than that.

BETTY: Just count yerself lucky I didn't say, 'Heard about the dead Avon lady lying in the grass going ding dong.

ENID. I can just picture Molly rolling about in her petunias gasping her last breath. (*She laughs; then*:) We mustn't be nasty though.

BETTY: They're not petunias, they're gladioli.

ENID: Are they?

BETTY: I only know 'cos my Carol told me.

ENID: It's all right for some, Molly got a ground-floor place and she hasn't got no kids, or disabled in the family.

BETTY: She always seems to know how to get everything.

ENID: Got a lot of mouth, Betty. Where's Ivy by the way?

BETTY: Up Florrie's. She's making a special effort this time. Florrie's got something to help her hear the telly better from the Social Services and Mum wants one.

ENID: What? Nanny-radar-ears-Taylor, her hearing's more sensitive than a bat's.

BETTY: It means you can still hear the telly when other people are talking in the room so I gather.

ENID: I wouldn't fancy them nosey do-gooders sniffing around.

BETTY: Mum can handle them.

ENID: Well, my Bob won't stand for it. He won't. I don't know exactly what he earns so he ain't going to relish the thought of blabbing it to someone else.

BETTY: Now I don't agree with that, Enid. We're living in modern times, bin years since we got the vote.

ENID: Oh he's never kept me short, Betty, you know that. I'm sure if I really knew it would only make for unpleasantness

BETTY: And they earn it. You can't expect a man to flog his guts out for nothing, I s'pose. They're entitled to their pleasure.

ENID: Not that that costs them anything. Not now. Mind, was a time when a packet of three meant going without tea.

BETTY: Don't I know, risks I've taken.

ENID: Me too.

BETTY: For the pleasure of one tea and one F in the same evening, I have a sixteen-year-old son.

ENID: Could've bin worse like me and had five kids.

BETTY: Now that was bad luck.

ENID: Bad luck?! I can tell you, Betty, if I'd 'ad me wits about me I'd 'ave sued Durex, I would, Featherweight and Gossamer my arse. I'd rather they were made outta bloody inner tube – safer.

BETTY: Maybe Bob didn't get the air outta them properly.

ENID: Didn't get the air outta them? Betty, they split so many times I threatened to take a pumice stone to his dong.

BETTY: Enid! Really!

ENID: Betty, it don't matter, no one can hear us. You know how they was invented, don't you? That John Wand used sheeps' innards.

BETTY: Load of tripe.

ENID: No, it's true.

BETTY: I was making a joke.

ENID: I know, so was I.

BETTY: Oh. (*She picks up TV remote control.*) See this? Do you see this?

ENID: Oh we've had one of them for ages, what about it?

BETTY: Look at it, just look at it, and think about contraceptives.

ENID: Do what? (*Pause.*) You mean hold it between your knees while he tries to get on top of you.

BETTY: They can make these two a penny but they can't make nothing better than Jonnies.

ENID: Well, they can't apply electronics to sheaths. You can't have a silicone chip in a condom, you daft apeth.

BETTY (*looking at the blank screen*): Hey, Enid, have you ever heard of the Common?

ENID: What are you insinuating?

BETTY: I mean, land, like park, common.

ENID: What, Clapham Common, Ealing Common, Wanstead Flats.

BETTY: No, on the telly. Some women living in caravans and tents and that because they don't want the bomb.

ENID: Oh yeah. It's called Greenham Common.

BETTY: What do you think of it?

ENID *pulls a face and puts her forefinger to her head to indicate that someone is mad.*

BETTY: Who is?

ENID: Those women, who else?

BETTY: That's the same face you pull at the thought of the government.

ENID: Who cares?

BETTY: But what was it about?

ENID: Betty this is boring.

BETTY: Tell me?

ENID: You should have heard my Bob going off about it.

BETTY: About what?

ENID: They desecrated the local war memorial. Bob was raging, carrying on about who was they to shit on our war dead, reckons people have had their throats cut for less.

BETTY: What you mean, desecrated it. Smashed it up?

ENID: No, I could have understood that. It was more spooky.

BETTY: Go on then.

ENID: Oh Betty, I don't know why you're so interested, they put little stones all over it.

BETTY: How d'you mean? Threw them at it?

ENID: No, just put them there.

BETTY: What on earth for?

ENID: According to them to remember all the people what copped it in Hiroshima but as Bob reckoned it puts a new meaning to getting stoned.

BETTY: Well I never.

ENID: I was just thankful he found his humour before he blew 'is gasket.

BETTY: But a lot of people must have died in Hiroshima.

ENID: Yeah, and if you'd have seen the telly you'd 'ave known. They collected a hundred or something.

BETTY: Jesus Christ.

ENID: I think they left him out of it. Anyhow, come to think, just shows how outta touch they are, everyone has Japanese tellies.

BETTY: Don't you care, Enid?

ENID: What about, war memorial? Stones? Japanese tellies?

BETTY: No, about the bomb.

ENID (*shrugs*): S'pose so.

BETTY: Then we should be grateful for what those women are doing.

ENID (*aggressive*): Should we? Should we? Should we really Betty?

BETTY: I only . . . I mean, don't take on, Enid.

ENID (*crossly*): How many bombs have we had dropped in our lives, Betty?

BETTY: We was only kids.

ENID (*angry*): Not that, how many times have we been at our wits' end? Eh? What about when you was evicted when your Carol was a baby and me with Linda — when she was really ill and the bloody doctor thought I was neurotic. In the end she had an operation which left a ruddy great hole in her back and it meant keeping her clean which meant washing her in the sink in a freezing cold kitchen. No hot water, nothing.

BETTY: All right, all right, we've had it tough. I didn't say we hadn't.

ENID: Do you want to know something, Betty, I'm glad, I'm really glad. They're all running scared with about as much direction as a chicken with its head cut off. Where were they when we were fighting for our kids' lives? If this is the only thing that threatens their lives then I'm glad.

BETTY: Enid, don't be so bitter. They might have had it rough and all.

ENID: Oh yeah, well I ain't joining in because I ain't protesting next to some posh woman so she can make sure her cut glass and Capo da Monte flowerpots are still intact.

BETTY: I thought you didn't care.

ENID: Huh. (*Pause.*) All I care about it having a laugh. I'm going back to me cooking, laughing all the way to teatime.

She goes out.

BETTY *opens her mouth to say something, sees the paper, picks it up but it's too late,* ENID *has gone.* BETTY *opens the paper to read an article.* IVY *enters.*

IVY: Blimey, just saw my Bob Big Gob flying across the balcony like a vulture outta hell.

BETTY: She only popped in for five minutes.

IVY: Giving it plenty of the bunny no doubt. Wonder she ain't got lockjaw.

BETTY: How was Florrie?

IVY: Pathetic. It's pathetic, Bet. If I ever get like that I'll drown meself in my commode.

BETTY: Well, you was with her long enough.

IVY: Made sure I ad a good butchers at that telly thing. I know what to say to the welfare now.

BETTY: Charming.

IVY: Oh, Florrie's okay, I feel sorry for her but once people start feeling sorry for you you've had it.

BETTY (*sarcastic*): What are you coming as, Ludovic Kennedy?

IVY: Enid upset you?

BETTY: No, we was talking.

IVY: She bragging about 'My Bob's antics again?'

BETTY: No.

IVY: Come on, I'll take a turn at that.

BETTY *puts a chair next to the ironing board and lowers it so* IVY *can sit and iron. Then she puts the kettle on.*

BETTY: Actually, we were talking about the bomb.

IVY: Oh, cheerful. Funny though, so was me and Florrie.

BETTY: Was you?

IVY: Florrie watches all the news every day. Well, she watches everything, can hardly get out of the chair. She puts on a big act when the social worker comes cause she don't want to go into a home.

BETTY: She'd be better off.

IVY: Course she wouldn't. Talk sense.

BETTY: What did she have to say?

IVY: She reckons if she had an address

she'd send a quid a week outta her pension to those women at that place, whatsit Common.

BETTY: Surely she don't approve of them?

IVY: It ain't that unbelievable, there ain't that many buggers who want to go up in a puff of smoke.

BETTY: But seems odd.

IVY: Got death in common ain't they? Florrie spends a lot of time worrying about death. State she's in it's hardly surprising.

BETTY: Enid reckons they was all worried about their china.

IVY: What does Enid know? She's never met them.

BETTY: I think she thought they were worried about their nice lives so they could go back and still have homes.

IVY: If they was worried about their lives they'd build a fall-out shelter. Anyhow they've left their homes — daft twit Enid is —

BETTY: But Enid . . .

IVY: Oh Enid, Enid, where has Enid bin all her life? Nowhere. Sometimes I think she just stepped out of Emmerdale Farm.

There is the sound of an outer door shutting.

BETTY: Hello? Jim? Jim? Is that you? Jim?

JIM *enters.*

JIM: Who do you think it was, King Kong?

IVY (*mutters*): Take your gorilla suit off then.

JIM: What she say?

BETTY: Nothing, nothing. Take no notice, Florrie upset her.

JIM: Florrie upset her? That's a laugh. She usually takes her do-it-yourself euthanasia kit round to upset Florrie.

BETTY: What?

JIM: Failing that, her mouth.

IVY (*who is ironing a shirt of* JIM's, *uses the iron with a vengeance*): I think I'll take these through.

IVY *gets up and exits with a pile of ironed clothes.*

BETTY: Jim, can't you be a bit more civil to Mum?

JIM: She's your mother. She doesn't have to live here.

BETTY: Now, Jim.

JIM: All right, Betty, but I always get the impression she's taking the rise outta me.

BETTY: I know she can be difficult.

JIM (*sees the paper*): What you got the *Sun* for?

BETTY: I didn't. Enid dropped in to return a fag she'd borrowed. She dropped it.

JIM: I do wish you wouldn't encourage her to come flapping round here every ten minutes.

BETTY: I didn't. I don't.

JIM: Anyway, listen, I've got some good news. I reckon I might be in with a chance of a full-time job at the garage.

BETTY: That is good news. Oh, that's wonderful.

JIM: Be a relief from all that cash in hand business. Mind, won't be for a couple of months. Don't bloody let it slip to that welfare officer.

BETTY: Course not. I am pleased, Jim.

JIM: Yeah well.

BETTY: Aren't you?

JIM: Oh yeah, I'm pleased. It's better than nothing, a lot better, but you know I spent seven years as a lad doing an apprenticeship. All my mates thought I was mad. They were earning much more than me. But it was worth it. Bet, I got a skill, I was proud of work, at the end of the day, I'd achieved something. I know I had ups and downs, changes of jobs, but I still felt something of worth. I was worth something. D'you understand what I mean?

BETTY: Yes. Yes I do.

JIM *goes out, to hang his coat up.*

JIM (*off*): And now what am I doing? Changing tyres — filling up cars with petrol. I tell you, Betty, even you could do that.

BETTY: Even me? Even me, who's mopped up after redundancies, unemployment, put you back on your feet again. Even me, who's done nothing of any worth except cook and clean and keep everything bloody together. Aren't I allowed to consider meself even a bit important?

JIM (*off*): What's that you say? Bet?

BETTY: NOTHING.

Scene Four

Monday afternoon. FIONA is at work. Interview room. Mud-splattered rucksack in the corner. She is on 'duty'.
MR GARDNER, a client sits opposite her. The desk is between them.

MR GARDNER: I know one thing, I've just about had enough. Darling, I'm telling yer don't sit there all smug wiv me girl cos that exactly how the other one, that wimpey geezer, started wiv me and he ended up wiv a chair over his head.

FIONA: I did not make your wife do anything, she did it of her own accord.

MR GARDNER: How come she never done it before then?

FIONA: She did go and stay with her mother once didn't she?

MR GARDNER: But she came back like a bloody shot.

FIONA (*pause*): Mr Gardner, you broke all the windows.

MR GARDNER: But she came back didn't she? That old cow always hated me, they bloody ganged up on me. Now stop beating about the bush and tell me where she is. I know my rights, she's my wife.

FIONA: I'm afraid I don't have the right to tell you. She knows where you are so I suggest you go home and wait for her to contact you.

MR GARDNER: Do yer? (*He becomes extremely angry.*) Do yer, darling, well I suggest you start to tell me where she is right this minute or . . .

MR GARDNER *leans across the desk.* LINDA *enters.*

LINDA: Christ, sorry . . . I thought you were on your own . . .

FIONA (*gives LINDA a look of panic so LINDA remains where she is*): Mr Gardner, I'm sorry but I've got other people to see . . . If you don't mind . . . (*She gestures towards the door.*)

MR GARDNER (*looks between them both, pause*): You haven't heard the end of this yet. I'll git you . . . You can't git one over on me, love, and don't think you will neither.

FIONA: Good afternoon, Mr Gardner.

MR GARDNER *goes out.*

LINDA: Rewarding afternoon?

FIONA (*sighs*): How lovely to see you.

LINDA: They told me you were on duty but they reckoned you'd be on your own.

FIONA: For a moment there so did I. (*Slight pause.*) What, you've been up to the office?

LINDA: Yeah, how d'you think I knew where you was?

FIONA: You didn't go up there with that badge on I hope.

LINDA: Unlike some I could mention I don't have two personas you know. If it's okay to go and hold hands down Greenham Common then it's okay to hold hands up the Mile End Road far as I'm concerned. How was it by the way?

FIONA: God, it seems like a million light years away, day I've had.

LINDA: Have you had time to find any disarming converts yet?

FIONA: It's not that easy you know, go marching into people's homes, saying, 'Date of birth, any problems? No? Good. By the way what are your views on peace camps?'

LINDA: I always told yer Social Services got a lot in common with the Gestapo, that's why they got the same initials.

FIONA: Don't start that up again. At least I don't work for a capitalist industry.

LINDA: Huh, I don't have the bloody choice, I wasn't lucky enough to get an education to escape my roots.

FIONA: Mine wasn't exactly handed me on a plate as you full well know.

LINDA: Granted. What was you saying about the converts?

FIONA: Only that it's difficult with all the shit that's going down in some people's lives for them to muster what's happening out there.

LINDA: Told yer. Anyway you haven't told me how you got on.

FIONA: I'm glad I went. Quite cold though. I missed you. What about you?

LINDA: Great time, didn't get up till six o'clock yesterday evening — then had breakfast in bed. It was really warm an' all.

FIONA: By the way your left wellie boot leaks.

LINDA: Really?

FIONA: And so I left them there.

LINDA: That's useful.

FIONA: This woman's right wellie boot leaked so I thought I'd donate them, is that okay?

LINDA (*agreeing*): Fine, now I've done my bit I can rest easy.

FIONA: Ah good, I'm glad I''ve caught you in an activist mood.

LINDA: Oh dear.

FIONA: I want you to come down with me, for the anniversary, before the eviction.

LINDA (*lightly*): What about all the people what get evicted round here? Who's fighting for them? I ain't going all the way down there for a bundle.

FIONA: You'll like it, I know.

LINDA: Why?

FIONA: Well . . . umm . . . because . . . because it's there . . . the space . . .

LINDA: I know it's an open space, so is Victoria Park.

FIONA: Naw, the space for . . . creativity . . .

LINDA: CREATIVITY?! Ha, Bourgeois crap.

FIONA: It's not, not altogether, well I liked it.

LINDA (*teasing*): Creativity? You? Your whole career is about control. What a load of rubbish.

FIONA: You can't be cynical all your life you know.

LINDA (*playing around*): Oh, goddess of creativity come down and cleanse my cynicism.

FIONA (*laughs*): Okay, okay, point taken.

LINDA: It's just that I want it to change more than war.

FIONA: Course it will. It's women only.

LINDA: Even so . . .

FIONA (*takes leaflet out of her jacket pocket*): Listen to this then. (*She reads.*) Apart from everything else . . .

LINDA: What's this? A bloody poetry reading?

FIONA: If I give it to you you won't bother to read it.

LINDA: I hope you ain't going to read the whole thing. I thought we were going out fer a meal.

FIONA: I'm only going to read two sentences.

LINDA (*lightly*): Okay wake me up when you've finished.

FIONA: Apart from everything else . . .

LINDA: You've said that once.

FIONA: Apart from everything else, authority, which is male oriented, is confused, bemused and deeply threatened by the growth and assertion of women working together in a different way. The women's peace camp is dealing with the tip of the iceberg . . . Cruise missiles, and at the same time, the base – patriarchy. (*She looks up.*) Well?

LINDA: I ain't going dancing naked through no woods painting myself with menstrual blood.

FIONA: But where's your creativity?

LINDA: In the bloody fish fryer. Come on, let's get out of here before another one of the Patriarchy's henchmen bursts in.

Scene Five

BETTY *and* ENID. *A month later.*

BETTY: I begun to think you'd emigrated.

ENID: Sorry, I've had a lot on me plate.

BETTY: I thought it was something I said.

ENID: Don't start up that war-mongering again.

BETTY: I wasn't.

ENID: We got enough bleedin' trials and tribulations of our own without taking on the world's.

BETTY: All right. I'm not going to say anything.

ENID: Well, aren't you going to ask what's wrong?

BETTY: Not if you don't want to talk about it.

ENID: Well, if you must know, our Kim got herself in the club again.

BETTY: Oh, Enid, I am sorry.

ENID: I don't see why any of us should be. She's not. Bob took on alarming about it.

BETTY: I can imagine.

ENID: I doubt that, Betty, I doubt if you can. Bob bellowing at her that she's always been a disgrace to the family since the day she got herself in trouble for the first time.

BETTY: Oh dear.

ENID: It weren't Bob though, it was her. She started screaming at him, 'How could I have got *meself* in trouble unless you're suggesting I'm the Virgin fucking Mary.'

BETTY: Enid!!

ENID: I'm only telling you what she said, Christ, I'd never say the Virgin fucking Mary in case I was struck down with lightning through the noonar and Linda, she's even worse than her you know. Oh yes. Three boys no trouble to me at all. Two daughters what are headstrong crackpots. Our Linda's barmy. Bob hates her.

BETTY: Oh Enid, she can't be that bad. She used to be such a wisecracker, takes after her mum.

ENID: Not anymore. I'm telling you, she's a po-face now. She's only got to see a bit of thigh on the telly and she goes mad, starts screaming, 'Sexist rubbish', and hitting the set with her garlic press thing.' I tell yer. Cracked. I told her, I said to her straight, I haven't lived through a world war to think the naked body's wicked.

BETTY: What she say to that?

ENID: Told me not to go over the top with the Alf Garnett act.

BETTY: She's not married yet then?

ENID: You're joking. Goes round wrecking marriages more like. I tell you, she's probably been more responsible for the divorce rate in this country than the Marriage Guidance Council. I haven't seen her since Christmas. Takes me six months to calm Bob down after she's bin. Just get him settled and what happens? The other one starts up. Anyhow what's bin going on with you?

BETTY: Nothing, nothing. Jim might be getting a proper job but otherwise nothing.

ENID: I wish our Dennis would do that. Gawd knows what he does but he gets paid a lot.

BETTY: Haven't you any idea?

ENID: Well, seems to be something to do with rollies.

BETTY: Cigarettes?

ENID: Yeah, every now and then he gives me a few and reckons save it and give yerself a treat. I kept 'em in me bag.

BETTY: You'd think if he earned that much he could buy his mum some decent cigarettes.

ENID: They're all right, as it happens. (ENID *takes out a couple of fags from an otherwise empty pocket – they are joints.*) Here, try one.

BETTY: No thanks. Let's have a look.

ENID: Smell a bit funny and they really ketch the back of your throat, but yer know beggars can't be choosers.

BETTY: Enid, I think these are drugs.

ENID: Naw, ther's no harm in them.

BETTY: I think this is pot.

ENID: NO. Dennis wouldn't have nothing to do with that. He fainted when he had his smallpox injection.

BETTY: These are illegal.

ENID: Oh Gawd, I smoked one in the doctor's surgery.

BETTY: Enid, I can't believe this. You've really let yourself go.

ENID: Oh I have, Betty, I have. These last few weeks.

She lights a joint.

BETTY: 'Ere you not going to smoke that in here?

ENID: Why not?

BETTY: S'pose the police bust in?

ENID: Betty, in all the years you've been alive have the police ever bust in to your front-room?

BETTY: But it's drugs.

ENID: It's nothing – try it, one puff.

BETTY: I think I should watch you in case you see purple elephants or try to fly out of the window.

ENID: Don't be ridiculous. If I could cook tea the day after me youngest was born, still shot through the eyeballs with pethidine, then a few dried tea leaves in a Rizla paper ain't going to bother me none. Come off it, Betty. Dennis would rip his own mother off. Sure as hell if it was proper drugs he wouldn't give me any. Try it.

BETTY: I'd rather not.

ENID: All right, don't. Never taken a risk in your life, Betty. Why start now?

BETTY (*grudgingly takes it*): You'd lead me to the gallows, you would.

ENID: Well?

BETTY: Don't feel any different.

ENID: Told you.

BETTY: What's that?

ENID: Where?

BETTY: I can see a big spider.

ENID: That's cos there is one. (*She bangs it with fag packet.*) Daft bat.

BETTY: Shame, I s'pose I wanted it to work and all.

ENID: Have you got anything to drink?

BETTY: Only some ginger wine left over from Christmas.

ENID: Get it out. Leave all the chores. Let's 'ave a game of cards, turn this place into a real den of Equity.

Lights change. There is a time lapse of about one hour.

BETTY *and* ENID *are playing cards. Although they don't realise it they are slightly stoned.*

BETTY: I bet you my electric cake knife.

ENID: You haven't got one.

BETTY: Well, I'm not going to lose.

ENID: Let's not play any more.

BETTY (*pushes cards aside*): Boring. Enid?

ENID: Come in Betty, I hear you.

BETTY: Enid, I want to tell you something.

ENID (*face lights up*): You've never had an organism.

BETTY: No. Something important.

ENID: Go on Betty. I'm receiving you loud and clear. Over.

BETTY: I'm bored.

ENID: Thanks a bundle. You don't exactly qualify as this estate's answer to Chas and Dave.

BETTY: Not you. I'm bored with my life, everything.

ENID: Buck up, wrestling on Saturday.

BETTY: That makes me more bored. Sometimes I don't feel I've done nothing with my life.

ENID: You haven't done nothing, you've taken drugs.

BETTY: As John would say 'big fucking deal'.

ENID: Yeah, no wonder Dennis is in so much trouble, selling things under false pretences. If I'd paid for this I'd sue him.

BETTY: I s'pose I feel a bit dizzy.

ENID: Same as smoking your first Woodbine. Let's face it, we've been spoilt by the filter tip.

BETTY: D'you think our mothers was bored?

ENID: 'Course not. Never had time. I blame machines, we got it easy, we got time to think . . .

BETTY: How bored we are.

ENID: Anyhow, we've done a lot. At least your kids are normal, look at me, my daughters seemed to have lost their trollies years ago and we moved from crappy Freedaman Street to modern places, that's not nothing.

BETTY: I wished we'd stayed now.

ENID: What, standing in a pile of rubble?

BETTY: No, like Beryl fought with the others in their street and they kept their places. Council put in all mod cons and all.

ENID: Spent years without hot water though, when we had that and baths and indoor lavs.

BETTY: And every day, every day, what have we got to show, eh? Just different foods to wash off the plates.

ENID: Get paper plates?

BETTY: Enid, sometimes I give up on you.

ENID (*sarcastic*): Oh hello, Bob.

BETTY (*stands up*): Can I show you something?

ENID: Well? As long as it's not your operation scar.

BETTY (*gets out old cereal packet and spills its contents of news cuttings on the table*): I'm collecting them.

ENID: What are they? Blimey, don't tell me you're the secretary to Errol Flynn's fan club all these years?

BETTY: No, look at them.

ENID (*glances at a couple*): Betty? These are about those silly women.

BETTY: I don't think it's that silly. Look, look, one woman has left her husband and five kids.

ENID: That's news?

BETTY: Says here, somewhere, that we're used to seeing men go off to war but we should get used to women going off for peace. Makes you think, doesn't it?

ENID: Does it?

BETTY (*collects them up, puts them back in the box*): Well, it made me think. If we're not going to use these weapons what's the point of having them?

ENID: They're a detergent against those who got 'em.

BETTY: Enid, you know the difference between a deterrent and a detergent.

ENID: In someone's face it would amount to the same thing.

BETTY: Aren't you worried at all?

ENID: Ain't bothered.

BETTY: Enid, sometimes you strike me as being as interesting as a piece of wet fish.

ENID: Oh do I? do I? Really? Well, I could tell you thinks that would make your hair curl.

BETTY: Oh yeah, you couldn't make a corkscrew curl.

ENID: Oh couldn't I? I'll show you, I tell you. I could make the hair in your nostrils curl.

BETTY: Go on then.

ENID: Oh no, you ain't getting anything to use on me.

BETTY: That's because the most daring thing you ever did was pinch a packet of fish fingers.

ENID: They was in a Hotpoint multi-freeze at the time though, don't forget. Tell you what we'll do – a phisological experiment.

BETTY: Pardon?

ENID: I saw it on telly just before *Maidenhead Unvisited.* Give us here that bit of that paper. Now, write down on it something you've never told no one.

BETTY: Enid, there was always something about your brain I couldn't fathom. That's because there's no depth to it.

ENID: Piss off and write it down. Go on.

Both write something on a bit of paper.

ENID: Now swap. (BETTY *looks at her paper again.*) What's the matter?

BETTY: Just checking the spelling. Okay.

They swap and read.

ENID: Betty!!

BETTY: Enid!!

ENID: God Almighty, I'll never be able to look her in the face again.

BETTY: Come to think, he don't look like the rest.

Both look at the papers again and start roaring with laughter.

JIM *enters.*

BETTY: Jim? Jim? Is that you Jim? Oh hello, Jim? Mum with you, Jim?

JIM: She's hanging her coat up, Bet. Bet. What's for tea?

ENID: Hot pot. (*She laughs.*)

JIM: If I was going to employ an au pair, Enid, you missed the boat by about forty years.

BETTY: Don't be ridiculous, Jim, child labour is against the law.

IVY *enters.*

ENID (*who, like* BETTY, *has been trying to control her giggles, bursts into laugher*): Oh hello, Mrs Taylor.

IVY: What's the matter, Enid, you just laid an egg?

She sits down and switches the telly on.

ENID: I ain't laid nothing lately except the table.

BETTY (*hisses*): Enid, Enid.

JIM: You're half cut.

BETTY: No, Jim, no we just finished off the bottle of Stones Ginger Wine, wasn't even half, was it, Enid?

ENID: Quarter, if that.

BETTY: Not even that, eggcup full, thimble.

ENID: It was off but it was a pity to waste it.

JIM: You never touch drink, what's the matter with you?

ENID: Celebration, Jim, anniversary, my Walter was divorced ten years ago today.

JIM: You celebrating that?

ENID: Celebration? Did I say celebration? I mean commiseration, you know, me always getting words wrong.

JIM: Silly great mare.

ENID: Broke my heart, we was drowning our sorrows.

Both women giggle.

JIM: You don't look too miserable to me. (*Pause.*) What's that smell?

BETTY: Shush.

JIM: Like burnt compost.

ENID: Indoor fireworks. I had them left over from Christmas.

JIM: Oh great, let's have a look. Is there a little gun?

BETTY: Chute.

JIM: Well they usually go puff puff. I haven't seen those since I was a boy.

BETTY: They're down the chute.

JIM: Betty, my dearest wife, the chute has been blocked for the past eighteen months.

ENID: Bin. They're in. The bin.

JIM: Hey, let's have a look, we can get 'em to work again with a couple of matches. John and I saw it on *Magpie.*

BETTY: No, no. Don't go rooting around in the bin, they're dead.

JIM: State you're in I'm surprised you can tell. (*He makes for the door.*)

BETTY: No, no, you wouldn't want to go down there. I emptied the commode in it.

JIM: You silly born bitch. What a stewpid thing to do. What you want to go and do a thing like that for? We'll have to treat the dustmen to take it away.

ENID: It will be a treat and all.

JIM: Are you going home or what?

ENID: On my way. Now remember Betty, you mustn't empty the pot in the bin agin.

BETTY: You don't mind if I don't get up, do you?

ENID: No dear, you've had a nasty shock.

ENID goes out.

JIM: Shock? Pot? Crackpot? She is. Living with her must be like hell with the lid off.

BETTY: Jim, I've bin thinking.

JIM: State you're in, find that a bit hard to swallow.

BETTY: Maybe I'll go down the chippy and get us tea.

JIM: Have you lost your head, it's not Friday.

BETTY: Make a change. Now what d'you want?

JIM: You're not going in that state.

BETTY: Mum, pop down the chip shop, will ya, I'll have a pie, saveloy and chips and an apple pie and perhaps a Mars Bar.

IVY: How can I? I'm housebound.

BETTY: Housebound? You're out so much you're practically a claustrophobic.

IVY: Yeah, well I might meet the social worker down there.

BETTY: Didn't see her playing bingo then?

CAROL *enters.*

JIM: I'll go but for goodness' sakes, pull yourself together woman.
(*To* CAROL:) Hello love, I'm just going down the chip shop, d'you want anything?

CAROL: No thanks, Dad, I can't stop long, I've left Joe-Joe with Darrel.

JIM: Plaice for you, Nan?

IVY: And chips.

BETTY: You can't have chips, you know full well they play havoc with your tracts.

JIM: Won't be long. (*He goes out.*)

CAROL: Hello, Nanny, Mummy.

BETTY: How many times do I have to tell you, I'm not bloody Tutankhamun reincarnated.

CAROL: Sorry, Mum.

BETTY: Nan, come on. You better have your bath while *Blue Peter* is on otherwise you'll leave it once you get stuck in front of that telly.

IVY: I hope you never get old, Carol. (*She gets up.*) Just as you look forward to a bit of peace and quiet the whole world gangs up and closes in on you.

IVY *goes out.* CAROL *sits next to* BETTY *who is staring out of the window. Silence.*

BETTY: Doesn't the sky look beautiful.

CAROL (*unnerved*): Yes, very pleasing to the eye, Mum, I'm sure.

BETTY: You know something a Sunday School teacher once told us?

CAROL: I never knew you went to Sunday School.

BETTY: Oh yes, your nan wanted us kids outta the house on Sunday afternoons. She had no more dignity or respect for the day of rest than a common streetwalker.

CAROL: Is that what the Sunday School teacher told you?

BETTY: No. Although it wouldn't surprise me if he was knocking her off.

CAROL: Mummy! Sorry, Mum! but really!

BETYY: No. This. Now tell me, can you imagine perfection?

CAROL (*pause*): Er, yes.

BETTY: What?

CAROL: Darrel's prize roses.

BETTY: Now can you imagine a man being able to make something perfect like a rose?

CAROL: No.

BETTY: Well, that's the theory. That logically there must be a God or at least something more capable than man.

CAROL: Must there? (*Silence.*) Well, if you say so.

BETTY: Though all these years I've bin thinking that there's got to be a flaw in it somewhere. If yer Nan had let me stay on and do my matric I was going to try and suss it out. (*Silence.*) Mind you, sometimes I look at the sky and think it's boring.

CAROL: Sometimes I look at Darrel's prize roses and think they're boring.

BETTY: Are you bored?

CAROL: 'Course not. I've got a beautiful home and little boy and a lovely husband.

BETTY: Huh, lovely husband. Which one is the little boy? I never forget when you came crying to me the first week back from your honeymoon when Darrel had thrown a tin of tomatoes at your head.

CAROL: Well they didn't actually hit my head and it was my fault, I didn't know he hated tinned tomatoes. And you were right. You sent me straight back and told me to make it work and I have but I'll always be grateful to you for that.

BETTY: 'No use crying over spilt milk Betty', that's what they should call me.

CAROL: Don't be silly. From that day to this, he's never so much as thrown a tin of baby food at me. Well, not so long ago he threw a hair brush but that was when McEnroe lost the Men's Open to Connors and there again I shouldn't have left it lying around on the settee.

BETTY: I mean some things get patched up and patched up but maybe we're all terrified of admitting that they're useless.

CAROL: Mum, what is the matter with you? I can't follow your train.

BETTY: Like you don't see old cars today that were around twenty years ago. Why? Because they don't work.

CAROL: Ah, but like you said, cars are manmade. Marriages are made in heaven.

BETTY: Marriages are made uneven.

CAROL: Don't say that, Mum.

BETTY: We don't even talk any more like we used to.

CAROL: What am I doing then? Singing *La Traviata*?

BETTY: And you try and speak posh all the time.

CAROL: Well, you know Darrel and his friends . . .

BETTY: Matter more than we do.

CAROL: No, but a silly thing of how you talk matters more to them that it does to you.

BETTY: And all those stupid parties you go to, Carol. They're just so boring and rubbishy.

CAROL: Oh, coming from you. They're no more boring than looking after Nanny or scheming with Enid all day on how to avoid the Avon lady. Sorry, sorry!

BETTY (*kindly*): Okay, nuff said. I'll put the kettle on. (*She gets up.*)

CAROL: Good idea. (*She picks up the notes on the table and proceeds to read them aloud whilst BETTY tries to conceal her panic.*) Dennis's real father is Mick the Masher of Bow Common Lane who's now serving time with the Kray Twins (?) (*Then:*) I married Jim on the rebound after I discovered my fiancé in bed with mum (?) Mother! What's this?

BETTY: Ah, not what you think. Ah, it was a silly game and not what you think at all. No. Enid and I were just saying how silly those stories were in *Woman's Weekly* and how we could write something better. Then we realised that we had such boring lives we couldn't. So we made up the most unlikely totally ridiculous thing possible. Pathetic, isn't it pathetic?

CAROL: Pathetic? It's macabre.

BETTY: It was dreadful, sick, fancy writing such a slanderous thing against your nan, even though it was a joke. If anything happens to her now I'll never forgive myself.

JIM *enters.*

BETTY: Ah, you're back. There you are, Jim. Nice to see you.

JIM (*sarcastic*): It's been so long my darling, have you missed me? Where's the old rooster?

BETTY: In the bath. Here, I'll put hers in the oven.

CAROL: Mum was just saying how fed up she is.

BETTY: Not now, Carol.

JIM: Should think she is. Sat on her arse all day yakking to Bible-basher Enid.

BETTY: Huh, Enid ain't as holy as you imagine.

JIM: No, she's a . . .

CAROL: Dad, you don't understand. Housework, same thing day in day out, gets monotonous.

JIM: Yeah, so does working.

CAROL: Apart from anything else, she can't go out to work because of Nanny.

JIM: Nanny, my armpit. She ain't exactly decrepit, you know. I'm sure if she can watch *Grange Hill* and still make the six-thirty bingo session she could probably get a job training Sebastian Coe.

BETTY: Oh I don't know. I just want something that matters to me.

JIM. Your husband and son don't matter of course.

BETTY: Yes they do. Where is John by the way?

JIM: Probably gone for a drink with the lads.

BETTY: Oh I don't know.

JIM: That's right. You don't know what you want, you're like the old lady who lived in the vinegar bottle.

BETTY: I want something to believe in.

JIM: Something to believe in. Hear that, Carol eh? That's a laugh. Coming from her. Someone who believes that you get pneumonia if your underwear isn't aired, that you mustn't walk under a ladder, or drop a knife or that you can get dirty diseases off a bog chain.

CAROL: Dad!

JIM (*thinking he's being funny*): I suppose God and the Labour Party aren't enough to believe in, eh, Bet?

CAROL: Mum?

BETTY: I feel a bit dizzy. I think I'll lie down for half an hour.

JIM: What about your dinner?

BETTY: I don't feel too good. I won't be long.

She goes out.

JIM: Gawd, she's never done that before.

CAROL: Dad, you know about, I mean, Mum, time of life the change.

JIM: Carol, I know all about women's troubles.

CAROL: I think, I think, now don't get cross. Sometimes Mum doesn't understand when you're making a joke.

JIM: She's out of practice, we haven't exactly 'ad a lot to laugh at lately.

CAROL: It's bin hard on her, you know.

JIM: Look, Carol, I might be able to get another job on the side, but don't mention that to Darrel mind, although it shouldn't be long before I get a full-time job. Then it'll be different, mark my words, I'll make it up to her. I'll see her all right.

Scene Six

BETTY's *kitchen. Several weeks later. JIM has been as good as his word. The kitchen is now sporting an electric toaster, liquidiser, microwave oven etc. ENID enters with a sheaf of daily papers.*

ENID: Blimey, it's getting to look like a regular Argos showroom in here.

BETTY: Yes.

ENID: Soon you'll be able to sit in a chair and press a button and everything will be done.

BETTY: Hasn't made much difference except now the toast pops up automatically burnt.

ENID: How can you be so ungrateful?

BETTY: I don't mean to be. I've tried talking to him, Enid, half these gadgets frighten me.

ENID: But he's trying, Betty. Gawd if I start saying I'm unhappy to my Bob he'd say count meself lucky or I will give yer something to be unhappy about. I'd be over the moon at all this, isn't even as if he's got a proper job yet.

BETTY: Enid, if you say to someone I'm cold and they set light to you do you think that's the answer?

ENID: Betty, I think you're a bit loola otherwise you bin listening to too much Radio Four. Anyway cheer up, I've got all the papers.

BETTY: Good, you know even Jim's had to think about it after seeing the Labour Party Conference on telly.

ENID: Well, I didn't half feel a twit asking for *The Times, Telegraph* and *Guardian.* Right, are we going to cut them up.

BETTY: It'll have to be later. Social worker's coming this morning.

ENID: I'll get out the way then. Don't want her analysing me, thanks very much. Where's Ivy?

BETTY: Trying to make herself helpless as possible.

ENID: Trying to undo the habit of a lifetime, must be some task. See you later then. (*She goes out.*)

IVY *enters.*

IVY: My Bob Big Gob done?

BETTY: Yes. Now, don't be rude to the social worker, we want something, remember?

IVY: Don't teach your grandmother to suck eggs. Anyone can fool that snipagig of a young do-gooder girl.

BETTY: Don't be so sure. I reckon they got as much power as the police if they got a mind — Jim calls them the caring branch of the SPG.

IVY: Ha, him. He couldn't control a fart in a bottle.

BETTY: Maybe not, but don't go telling her you got paralysed from the waist down in a bomb scare 'cos they might be stupid but they got access to doctors' records.

IVY: Na, they don't understand arthritis either, to them it's just another word what means old.

The doorbell rings.

BETTY: Remember when in doubt keep stum. (*She opens the door.*)

FIONA: Hello, my name's Fiona, I'm from the Social Services. I wrote and told you I was coming.

BETTY: Yes, do come in. Would you like a cup of tea?

FIONA: No, thanks very much.

BETTY: Well, do sit down.

FIONA (*sits, so does* BETTY): Thanks, how are things?

BETTY: You know, mustn't grumble but mother's not getting any better.

FIONA: I'm sorry to hear that. Hello Mrs Taylor, how are you feeling today?

Silence.

BETTY: Hearing's not so hot.

FIONA: Really? There wasn't anything on the file.

BETTY: Ears like everything else don't improve none with age.

FIONA (*stands in front of* NANNY *mouthing and shouting*): Mrs Clayton was saying your hearing has deteriorated.

IVY (*to* BETTY): What she say?

BETTY (*gesturing*): She said you're a bit deaf. Worried about deaf.

IVY: Death, of course I am. Nobody wants to die, do they, dear?

BETTY: Not death. Deaf, deaf.

FIONA: Have you seen your GP for a hearing aid?

BETTY: Oh no, she don't have one. Never bin one for human conversation, you might say. What she misses most is hearing the telly.

FIONA: We do have a special device, I might . . .

BETTY: Works like headphones?

FIONA: I think that's right.

IVY: Like Mrs Appleton's got at number seven?

FIONA *turns round.*

IVY: I've got the same trouble in me back as Mrs Appleton. We was comparing ourselves other day. Very bad legs.

FIONA: That's nice. How do you manage to see her? She's housebound like yourself.

BETTY: Er, my husband if he's not 'ad too 'ard a day carries her up the road.

IVY: What you say?

FIONA (*shouting*): She said her husband often takes you.

IVY: Keep your filthy assanations to yerself.

BETTY: Nice company for her them both being in the same boat — deaf like.

FIONA: Now, I was wondering about the possibility of a day centre.

BETTY: I don't think she'd like that.

FIONA (*mouthing, shouting*): Would you like to try going to a day centre?

IVY: I ain't setting foot in no play school for geriatrics.

FIONA: They do some lovely things, light factory work, basket weaving.

IVY: I ain't bloody blind.

BETTY: What she's trying to say is that she'd miss *Afternoon Plus* too much.

IVY: At least I don't shit meself like that load of cabbages up at the play centre.

BETTY: Mother. (*To* FIONA:) She's rambling. She gets like this. Take no notice.

FIONA: But she is usually quite lucid?

BETTY: Oh no. Her bowels are her strongest point.

IVY: When I was in hospital, the Sister says to her, your mother is marvellous. There's not a blemish up her back passage, didn't she, Bet, what did . . .

BETTY: Mum.

FIONA: That's nice, well it seems like we've got to the bottom of the matter, ha ha, yes. How, how is John these days? Is he enjoying the YOPS course?

BETTY: Seems to be, we don't see much of him. You know out and about but they're like that when they're young, aren't they?

FIONA: And is your husband still out of work?

BETTY: Er yes, but he's not here at the moment because he's doing the shopping. Gets on men's nerves hanging about the house all day.

FIONA: Can get on women's nerves as well. No troubles with the DHSS?

BETTY: Not so far. I mean, giros arrive on time and that.

FIONA: That's one thing.

BETTY: You ain't the same as them are you?

FIONA: No way. We call them the Department of Stealth and Total Obscurity.

BETTY (*unaware that this is a joke*): Oh really, we call it the Social. .

FIONA: Well. (*She gets up.*) No other worries?

BETTY (*lightly*): Except the bomb.

FIONA: Not much Social Services can offer there.

BETTY (*trying to be casual*): Er, have you ever heard of that err peace camp thing in the south?

FIONA: Greenham Common?

BETTY: Yes, I expect you think those kids should be in care. What with them going to prison and that.

FIONA: No, I don't think that at all.

BETTY: You don't think they're mad?

FIONA: No, what do you think about it?

BETTY: I've bin trying to follow it.

FIONA: Have you?

BETTY: Well, you know what I've seen on the telly and that. Do you know anyone what's actually bin there?

FIONA: I have, as a matter of fact.

BETTY: What's it like?

FIONA: Like it is on the telly only colder.

BETTY: You know all the other women?

FIONA: Not really, no.

BETTY: Are they all well off and that?

FIONA: No, all sorts of backgrounds.

BETTY: I read in the paper that one woman was a doctor.

FIONA: That's true.

BETTY: But I s'pose that's the sort of thing the papers would pick up on.

FIONA: Yes, I s'pose it is.

BETTY: Still, I can't keep you standing chatting all day, you must be busy.

FIONA: That's okay. (*She takes what is now a crumpled piece of paper from her pocket.*) This is a sort of handout leaflet. D'you want it?

BETTY: Are you sure?

FIONA: Of course.

BETTY (*takes it*): Thanks . . . I've been sort of saving news cuttings.

FIONA (*searches her bag*): Hang on — there's something about it in this magazine. You can have it, I've read it.

BETTY: That's very kind.

FIONA: I'm very pleased that you're interested.

BETTY: So am I. Pleased that you are I mean.

FIONA: I've got some other stuff at home, I'll bring it with the gadget for the telly.

BETTY: Thanks very much.

FIONA: Nice to meet you. (*She goes out.*) Bye.

BETTY: And you. Bye.

IVY: What was that all about?

BETTY: You know full well. You won't go telling Jim now, will you?

IVY: Betty, you've got to stick up for yourself. Look at the way he creates about me going to Bingo but there's nothing he can do about it. What should it matter to him what you talk about — to her or for that matter to that silly born banana Enid.

BETTY: She can't help getting her words mixed up.

IVY: She can. She does it for a laugh. She just ain't grasped the fact that you're s'posed to take the Michael outta someone else not yourself.

There is the sound of a door shutting.

BETTY (*hides the magazine and slips the piece of paper inside a copy of* Woman's Realm): Jim? Jim? Is that you, Jim?

JIM *enters.*

JIM: No, it's Omar Sharif returning to his harem.

BETTY: You just missed the social worker.

JIM: Did she want to know where I was?

BETTY: I told her you was shopping.

JIM: Did she believe you?

BETTY: Yes, she didn't take it in and we fooled her and got one of those things for the telly.

Silence. JIM *switches on the telly.* BETTY *reads the piece of paper* FIONA *gave her, between the covers of* Woman's Realm. *A long pause.*

BETTY (*without thinking*): Jim, what's patriarchy mean?

JIM: Do what?

BETT: What's patriarchy?

JIM: Who? What are you reading?

BETTY: Nothing. It's in this magazine.

JIM: Let's have a look. What's the sentence?

BETTY: It's a recipe for a patriarchy cake.

JIM: A patriarchy cake? What in hell's name . . .?

BETTY: What does it mean?

JIM: No idea. (*Pause.*) Hang on. Hierarchy is like boss at the top — then the deputy's under him, then under them, then at the bottom the workers.

BETTY: How d'you mean?

JIM: Like a triangle with the boss at the top and all the workers along the bottom, but funny name to call a cake.

BETTY: Maybe it's in the shape of a triangle.

JIM: Well, I'm certainly looking forward to eating it.

IVY (*looks up*): So am I.

Scene Seven

The next day. BETTY *is sitting at the table with both the October edition of* Sanity *magazine and the paper.* ENID *enters. There are three jam-centred swiss rolls on the table.*

ENID: Coast clear? Where's Nanny?

BETTY: Cutting her toenails, chiropody's non-existent round here now. Enid? What does patriarchy mean?

ENID: A sort of parrot disease.

BETTY: I don't know why I bothered to ask.

ENID: What on earth d'you want to know that for?

BETTY: I haven't got time to go into it all. But you know that welfare worker that came yesterday?

ENID: Not personally no.

BETTY: She gave me this paper all about it.

ENID: About welfare workers.

BETTY: No. The women's peace camp.

ENID: Social Services are telling people about that, blimey, as if they haven't got enough work to do.

BETTY (*impatient*): No, like it just cropped up in the conversation.

ENID: I reckon they must be real lonely, wanting to spend the whole day inflicting themselves on folk and bending their ears off.

BETTY: Listen, anyway I asked her but then I asked Jim what it meant by mistake because then he asked where I read it so I told him it was a cake recipe so now he wants to eat patriarchy cake.

ENID: Oh I see, clear as mud.

BETTY: Are you going to help me or not?

ENID: I don't see how I can, I can't

understand a word you're on about.

BETTY: It's this bit. (*She reads*:) We are dealing with the tip of the iceberg. Cruise missiles and at the same time the broad base patriarchy.

ENID: I don't see what I can help with. I s'pose Cruise missiles are the bomb, broad base — like a flan case I suppose.

BETTY (*tracing a line with her finger*): This is a tip.

ENID (*looks round*): Well, could do with a hoover.

BETTY: No, look. (*She traces another line.*) This is the base. Jim reckoned it must be like hierarchy which is like a triangle. Now it's a case of sticking these Swiss rolls together and cutting the edges in the triangle.

ENID *picks one of the Swiss rolls up and gives an impression of Groucho Marx.*

Can't you ever be serious?

ENID: Me? Me? Here you are, making a God knows what cake.

BETTY: Patriarchy.

ENID: And you don't even know the meaning of the word. Me, me. You know something, Betty, if anyone's losing their marbles, it's you.

BETTY: Wait a minute.

ENID: What, for the men in the white coats?

BETTY: What did Steptoe call his father?

ENID: A dirty old man.

BETTY: No, when he was trying to be posh.

ENID: Dirty old basket.

BETTY: Pater.

ENID: Oh yeah, always thought that was funny, his name was Albert.

BETTY: Tut. It means father.

ENID (*sarcastic*): Oh what a relief.

There, you've solved it. Father triangle, that's what it means. Father Christmas, Father Time and Father Triangle. Christianity, Timearchy and Patriarchy.

BETTY: Maybe that's it. God the Father, he's at the top.

ENID: I thought you reckoned the bomb was at the top.

BETTY: I just don't . . .

ENID: I believe in one God, God the Father, God the Bomb and God the Holy Patriarchy Cake.

BETTY: Enid, don't say that.

ENID: Anyhow, three Swiss rolls stuck together aren't going to fool Jim.

BETTY: I'll cover it with icing, he won't know.

ENID: I bin thinking.

BETTY: Don't strain yourself.

ENID: You know when I got the papers this morning, Betty, they'd had another brick through the window.

BETTY: Not again. Poor souls.

ENID: And I was sort of thinking like, what would they think about all this peace camp business. Petrol through the letter box every other night. Never knowing if they'll all be burnt in their beds. What are they going to worry about a bloody missile for, probably welcome it dropping on them bastards, I would.

BETTY: I thought you weren't bothered about them.

ENID: Got me thinking, Bet, we think we've 'ad it hard.

BETTY: We don't know the half.

ENID: Maybe like those women have got nothing really to do with us.

BETTY: Oh no. Then look at this. (*She points to* Sanity *magazine.*)

ENID: Sanity? At least you recognised your problem, Betty, you ain't got any. Where'd you get it?

BETTY: Social worker gave it to me.

ENID: She thought you was insane as well.

BETTY: No, no, it's about . . .

ENID (*picks it up, opens it*): The Church and the bomb. We weren't wrong, Betty, it's in here.

BETTY: No look here. Here. Those women went to prison for what they believed.

ENID: Well, my Dennis bin sent down fer what he believed in, just so happens that the judge's beliefs was not in accordance wiv his.

BETTY: And one of them reckons she was the sort of person who just made the tea for other people before she got involved.

ENID: Well?

BETTY: I've made lots of tea.

ENID: She means at meetings, you don't do that.

BETTY: But I could describe my life as making tea for others.

ENID: This thing's obsessed you, you're obsessed. You'll be making tea for others in the nuthouse the way you're carrying on. Either that or Holloway bloody prison.

BETTY: Did you see in the evening paper about them lying down in the road up Westminster?

ENID: I said to Bob I said. They're asking for it. Pretending to be dead then a bloody great bus will run 'em over and nobody will know the difference.

BETTY: Everybody thought the suffragettes were mad at the time.

ENID: Oh no, you ain't bin to see another boring exhibition down the library?

BETTY: I bin thinking about it. Remember them letters, from the Labour MPs? Even they thought it was disgusting that women should 'ave the vote.

ENID: Yeah well, it didn't change much.

BETTY: Maybe 'cos people forgot about it what with the war and that.

ENID: Anyway, you'd better get on with this daft cake. One thing they never forgot in a hurry is their stomachs.

BETTY: You going to give me a hand?

ENID: Don't worry, if it turns out okay I'll make Bob one. Never know, eating patriarchy cakes could becomes like Pancake Day.

IVY enters.

ENID: Hello Mrs Taylor, are your feet any better?

IVY: Yeah, I'm just off to audition for the Sugar Plum Fairy.

ENID: Second thoughts I think I'd better get along.

The doorbell rings.

BETTY: Who can that be?

ENID: I'll get it. (*She opens door to a man.*)

MR SMITH: Good morning, madam, I'm from the Department of Health and Social Security.

ENID: Hello and goodbye.

MR SMITH: Actually I wanted a word with your husband.

ENID: He don't live here.

MR SMITH: Oh, this is . . . (*He looks at his file.*)

BETTY: Please come in, this is a friend of mine who was just leaving.

ENID: Like I said, hello and goodbye.

MR SMITH: Oh . . . Hello Mrs Clayton, is your husband at home?

BETTY: No, who are you?

MR SMITH: I'm from the Department of Health and Social Security.

IVY: We had a visit from you lot yesterday.

MR SMITH: Really, I wasn't informed.

BETTY: About an aid for the TV.

MR SMITH: That must have been Social Services, I'm from Social Security.

BETTY: Oh it is good of you to come, we only put in for a heating allowance for mum a few weeks ago.

MR SMITH: It's not about that I'm afraid. Could you tell me where your husband is.

IVY: He's babysitting for his daughter.

MR SMITH: When will he be back?

IVY: Not sure. She had a hospital appointment, you know what they're like. Why?

MR SMITH: We have reason to believe that he is in fact working.

IVY: Whatever gave you that idea?

MR SMITH: We received a letter stating details.

BETTY (*shocked*): From who?

MR SMITH: We're not permitted to divulge its source even if we knew it.

BETTY: You mean to say someone wrote you a poisonous pen letter and you believed them?

MR SMITH: You'd be surprised how reliable they are.

BETTY: Well, that's funny 'cos if anyone gets one in the post the police usually advise you to throw it away but I s'pose they tell you to believe it.

MR SMITH: Not exactly but we have to check these things out.

IVY: Well, he ain't working and that's that. Now what about my heating allowance?

MR SMITH: I'm not sure if this family is entitled to Social Security. I'm afraid I can't apply for a heating allowance until I find out definitely whether your son-in-law is working.

IVY: By which time it'll be the middle of December and I'll have kicked the bucket with hypothermia.

BETTY: Mum.

MR SMITH: I'll make a note of it. Now, you're Mrs Taylor, Mrs Clayton's mother?

IVY: No I'm her pet snake.

MR SMITH: And what makes you think you're entitled to a heating allowance?

IVY: You wiley bastard.

BETTY: Mum! (*To* MR SMITH:) She don't know what she's saying.

IVY: Oh yes she does. She knows what he's saying and all, he means we have to make a guess at what would qualify us for a heating allowance and if we guess right we can have it. Well have I got news for you mate – this ain't family fortunes. For one thing, I'm always cold. I have to have a fire on even in the summer and all night in my room in the winter. I've got chronic arthritis and I'm very weak – for Chrissake, I'm a dying woman.

MR SMITH: We're none of us getting any younger, ha ha.

IVY: No and you won't be getting any older if you don't take that sneer off your mush.

MR SMITH: I would remind you I'm here to investigate a possible fraud by the claimant of this household. I do not take kindly to being threatened within inches of my life. I will look into the heating allowance but, mark my words, not until we've investigated the other matter thoroughly.

BETTY: Thank you for coming.

MR SMITH: Good day, Mrs Clayton.

BETTY: Umm, have you heard of Greenham Common as well?

MR SMITH (*thinks by now the whole household is mad*): As well as what? What about it?

BETTY: I just wondered what you thought.

MR SMITH: It's nothing to do with me I'm sure, but no doubt some of them are extracting state benefits under false pretences. We're probably having a field day down there. Good day.

He goes out.

BETTY: Oh dear.

IVY: To think people died in the war for the likes of that cretin to breed.

BETTY: You realised you went too far I s'pose, Bette Davis. Well, you're not going to get an Oscar for that performance.

IVY: What are you going to get 'It was nice to meet you' Betty, when are you going to stand up for yourself, eh? People like that are scum of the earth, they don't deserve the time of day.

BETTY: No, mother, people what wrote that letter are the scum of the earth. Mind, he didn't like the idea of Greenham Common much.

IVY: I hope it drops on the bloody lot of 'em, put pay to the likes of him, that'll teach him a lesson he'll never forget.

JIM enters.

BETTY: Oh Jim, something terrible's happened.

JIM: Nanny's dentures fallen down the bog again?

BETTY: No, sit down, sit down. Man from Social Security's been round, they know you're working.

JIM: Know? They can't know.

BETTY: Well, someone's s'posed to have written a letter ain't they?

JIM: What? What bastard?

BETTY: I don't know. What are we going to do?

JIM: You didn't tell them nothing?

IVY: We never. We carried on about we thought it was for the heating allowance.

BETTY: Who could have done that?

JIM: Nobody knew about it. Wait a minute. I know who it was, Enid, that's who.

BETTY: No, Jim, no. She wouldn't.

JIM: Want a bet, I never want her in here again.

IVY: Jim, I ain't never had a lot of time for the woman but I don't think it could've bin.

JIM: We'll see, if she has the audacity to show her boat again, but my bet is she'll lay low for a couple of weeks and, as far as I'm concerned, for ever.

Scene Eight

LINDA *and* FIONA's *squat.* LINDA *is cutting up pieces of card so that it makes a stencil. (We can't see what it reads.)* FIONA *enters with shopping bag.*

LINDA: Hi.

FIONA: Hi, got the paint.

LINDA: Great. Did you remember the spaghetti?

FIONA: What do we need that for?

LINDA: Tea?

FIONA: Oh hell, sorry I forgot.

LINDA: Don't matter. No problem.

FIONA: Sorry.

LINDA: S'okay. Are you all right?

FIONA (*flatly*): Yeah. Went to see Betty today.

LINDA: Thought you were pleased about that. Certainly proved me wrong.

FIONA: She seemed . . . well . . .

LINDA: She gone off the idea of going down there, then eh?

FIONA: Not exactly. Have you?

LINDA (*smiles*): A deal's a deal. So what was Betty pissed off about?

FIONA: She seemed more preoccupied

with some sort of misunderstanding she'd had with your mum.

LINDA: Perhaps we should get together and form a club. Non-effective direct discussion we've had with Enid.

FIONA: It seems to have really got to her.

LINDA: Did you manage to get out of her what it was all about?

FIONA: The fraud squad have been round there. And Betty's old man thinks your mum grassed them up.

LINDA: My mum, whatever else she might or might not do, would never do that, not in a million years, never.

FIONA: Apparently she hasn't been round there since.

LINDA: Why ever not?

FIONA (*shrugs*): They assume guilty conscience.

LINDA: Didn't you go and talk to Enid?

FIONA: How could I? Apart from the fact that my job description doesn't involve peace-making between neighbours, I find the whole concept fraught with Freudian tension.

LINDA: What you on about?

FIONA: I don't relish the thought of case work with your mother.

LINDA: Oh dear. It looks like I'll have to do a mother-daughter reunion number.

FIONA: It wouldn't come amiss. You haven't been home for months.

LINDA: Paternal problem patterns.

FIONA: Do what?

LINDA: Uses his kids as a target practice against life's frustrations. Kicked me down three flights of stairs once.

FIONA: My mum used to belt us when we were kids.

LINDA: Yeah, I s'pose I was only twenty-three at the time.

FIONA: How does Enid get on with him?

LINDA: She gets on my nerves. Basically, she weaves a web of complete fabrication round everything. She refers to the stair episode as that time your father was helping you down the stairs.

FIONA: Surely she doesn't believe it.

LINDA: Well as time goes on they get even more modified. Till every action he does becomes bloody saintly.

FIONA: Don't you ever get to talk to her on her own?

LINDA: Rarely, then she's on edge in case he comes through the door. Oh, she won't have a word said against him. The most that ever gets admitted, is that they've had their ups and downs but that's followed immediately by, if she ever had her life again she'd marry him again. Mind you she does say it parrot fashion and at breakneck speed like she might be struck dead at any moment for such an enormous lie.

Silence.

FIONA: What d'you think it would take for Betty and Enid to change their lives?

LINDA (*pause. Smiles*): A bomb?

Scene Nine

IVY. *Monologue.*

IVY: When you see old people on the telly in those comedy programmes what are made by morons and aren't at all funny, all they ever seem to open and shut their traps about is the war. Everybody's fed up to the back teeth with the bloody boring war. You know all that British Legion stuff about, 'I died in the war for you' and being proud that half their relatives got splattered all over the shop for a better nation and once in a while you gets round to thinking that this is the better nation and it's the sort of thought that's so depressing you don't want to get round to thinking it again for a few years.

We had a great time round here in the war. Yeah, I know you're thinking, 'And the silly old crow's going to tell us it brought us all together'. Course it brought us together. Half the bloody streets disappeared. Every Saturday there was a party 'cos you didn't know which house would be flattened next. One day we'd be having a knees-up and the next the place would be a pile of dust. Women became strong. We had to be. We ran the country and when it was over we could see the way things were going and that it was a bit late for us but we invested our dreams and hopes and plans in our daughters only to see them evaporate like pee in the lift on a hot day. Having kids is important but having a washing-machine, a television and a car became more important. And a husband with a steady job was set up as number one main aim. Bloody silly values for a country what was s'posed to be embarking on freedom, that's all I can say. The war's so bloody boring because what did it change for the better? For us, seems like sod all.

Scene Ten

CAROL *and* BETTY.

CAROL: All this time, I can't believe it.

BETTY: We walked past each other on the stairs never said a word.

CAROL: Is the lift broken again?

BETTY: On and off, I won't get in it in case I get stuck.

CAROL: Forget it, Mum, if Enid wants to act like that let her, you've got enough worries and I'm sorry to say but it proves it must have been her.

BETTY: No Carol not Enid. Anyhow your dad's been employed properly,

well three days a week w[...] insurance is better than n[...]

CAROL: It's a pity you had [...] of all those things to pay b[...] Social Security.

BETTY: I didn't want them in the first place.

CAROL: But dad cares, he could have spent the money on himself.

BETTY: He doesn't listen, he's never listened to me or what I want.

CAROL: What do you want?

BETTY: I don't know.

CAROL: How can he understand that if you don't?

BETTY: Anyway, that's enough of me moaning on, how are you and Darrel?

CAROL: Oh, fine. (*Pause.*) Listen, Mum, you remember before I was married?

BETTY: When you was courting.

CAROL: As you'd put it, yes. You know we used to come back here when you and Dad had gone to bed.

BETTY: Carol, love, there's no need to go into that. I know, I know young people these days well, like to make sure they're well suited before . . . (*Then she adds quickly:*) they get married.

CAROL (*laughs*): No, Mum, not that.

BETTY: Oh, well that's a relief.

CAROL: We used to have a real laugh. Darrel used to line up all your ornaments on the floor and describe them as though it was an auction — go into detail — orange plastic ashtray.

BETTY: It was that funny?

CAROL: I used to laugh, Mum, but inside it was sad, I used to think, I still do, this collection of trinkets is all my mum's got to show for her life. I swore I'd never be like you.

BETTY (*quietly angry*): Carol, I never wanted posh things, I didn't want anything else. I know this place might seem like a pile of tawdry crap to you and your friends but that's their problem. I don't want to have to go tripping round antique china or freeze to death with pine-stripped floorboards for that matter.

CAROL: I didn't mean to upset you. I was trying to explain.

BETTY: A lot of this stuff was bought for me from you and John when you were kids, surely that's more important than a Rembrandt painting?

CAROL: Yes, but it boils down to nothing.

BETTY: Is that what you wanted? A posh home, posh car, posh husband, because that's exactly what you got. What does that boil down to, eternal bliss, eh? Cos you don't seem none too ecstatic to me.

CAROL: I didn't want to be like you. I wanted a husband with prospects, a home with a garden and kids, kids who would grow up with all the things I never had, but no I'm not happy.

BETTY: You and me ended up the same — we both don't know what we want.

CAROL: What else is there?

The doorbell rings.

BETTY: The doorbell. (*She gets up and answers it.*) Hello.

LINDA: Hello, I don't know if you remember me, I'm Linda, Enid's daughter.

LINDA *enters.*

BETTY: You remember Carol, you used to go to school together.

CAROL (*forced smiles*): Linda, how are you these days?

LINDA: Okay thanks and you?

CAROL (*rather abrupt*): I'm married now.

LINDA: I'm not.

BETTY (*pleased*): You always got on so well together.

LINDA: Umm, look I've come round because I think there's been a misunderstanding. Mum was a bit afraid to come.

BETTY: Huh, I don't believe Enid's afraid of anything.

LINDA: It seems that someone tipped the DHSS off about your husband working and you thought it was Mum.

BETTY: Actually, no. Jim thought it was.

LINDA: Well, it appears the same day someone came round to investigate my brother Dennis's illegal working habits and my dad thought it was you.

BETTY: Why didn't Enid tell me?

LINDA: Because you've been avoiding her. What was she to think?

BETTY: Where is she?

LINDA: Pacing the balcony like something out of a John Wayne movie.

BETTY: Hang on a second. (*She goes out.*)

CAROL *and* LINDA *are left alone. There is an awkward silence.*

CAROL: I've got a little boy now.

LINDA: That's nice.

CAROL: I don't s'pose you really think that.

LINDA: Why not?

CAROL: I remember the things you used to say at school.

LINDA: I remember the things you used to say.

CAROL: You were always getting me in trouble.

LINDA: Really? I thought that was Darrel.

CAROL: Well, I've changed.

LINDA: So I see. What d'you mean me? You were the one. It was me who took the rap because you looked as though butter wouldn't melt in your mouth.

CAROL: I suppose you're one of those lot at Greenham Common.

LINDA: Actually, I'm the chief fish fryer at Littlewoods canteen. I would have thought women's peace camps were more your bag than mine.

CAROL: You're joking.

LINDA: Don't you want a world for your little boy to grow up in?

CAROL: Actually we're thinking of emigrating to Australia.

LINDA: Oh, that's nice.

CAROL: I know you don't think that for one moment.

LINDA (*shrugs*): Been some good Australian films on the telly recently.

CAROL: And I suppose you're a vegetarian.

LINDA: 'Fraid so.

CAROL: Huh, I remember the time you pulled the tail off the mouse in the biology lab.

LINDA: That was an accident. I remember you told me not to worry it would grow another and you believed it.

Both laugh. Then there is an embarrassed pause.

CAROL: Don't mention anything about cross-country running.

LINDA: What cross-country running? We spent the whole time . . .

CAROL: I said don't mention it.

LINDA: Mum's the word.

BETTY *and* ENID *enter*.

CAROL (*to* LINDA. *Put down*): Funny how we haven't got anything in common any more. (*Then to* BETTY:) Hello Mum, everything all right?

ENID: Bleedin' stupid nanas we've been.

BETTY: Yes, we sorted it out.

ENID: Take me the rest of my life to sort Bob out though. Thanks to you, madam.

LINDA: He started it.

ENID: And you, you had to retaliate didn't you, couldn't keep your trap shut.

LINDA: When someone bellows in your lughole, 'You filthy bleedin' perverted . . .'

ENID (*cuts her short*): Yes well, your father's tolerance of you has been stretched to the limits.

LINDA: So has mine.

BETTY: Let's all have a cup of tea.

ENID: You're on the road, Bet, it starts with cups of tea at meetings.

LINDA: What you on about, Mum?

ENID: Never you mind.

BETTY: Tell her, Enid, she might know something about it.

ENID: Here we go. Have you heard of the women's peace camp at Greenham Common?

LINDA: No, what's it about?

ENID: You must have. Everyone has.

BETTY: Been on the telly, everything.

LINDA: Yes, I have.

ENID: See, that's typical of her, contradiction is her middle name.

LINDA: I wouldn't choose a middle name with dick in it, thank you.

ENID: Well, what did you say no for then?

BETTY: Enid, don't carry on at her.

ENID: Typical Betty that is. (*To* LINDA:) Well you know something, Betty's possessed by it.

BETTY: I'm only interested.

ENID: And I became the research worker. In fact, I reckon I should apply to the GLC for a grant.

BETTY: Oh, Enid.

ENID: What that means, is, I went to get the high class papers. What Betty was too embarrassed to.

LINDA: What do you think about it?

ENID: Me? Well, you know me, Linda, I think people what value their lives are worthless.

LINDA: I weren't aware you thought your life was insignificant.

BETTY: Take no notice, Linda. Even Enid's admitted to thinking.

CAROL: What I want to know is why there are no men there?

BETTY: Oh, I'd never thought about that.

CAROL: Why does it have to be women only? That's a bit sexist isn't it, Linda?

ENID: Oh, the men would only spoil it.

LINDA: It was set up on women's initiatives, Carol. There are very few things women can call their own in this society.

BETTY: Because of the patriarchy.

CAROL: The what?

ENID: Ah, don't you know what that means?

CAROL: Do you?

ENID: We know all about it and we know what the opposite is an' all; matriarchy, and even though that's been extinct for a few thousand years, me and Betty is raising it from the dead.

BETTY: I wouldn't say that, Enid.

ENID: What would yer say then?

BETTY: Well, it's certainly buried round 'ere, but it ain't exactly dead.

LINDA (*interested*): What do you know about . . .

ENID. All I know is, if I don't get Atilla the Hun's tea within the next two seconds I'm going to be a gonner meself. Now listen girl, don't go leaving it another few thousand years before you condescend ter drop in again.

LINDA: Mum, how can I wiv him? Why don't you come and see me?

ENID: I ain't setting foot in no commie squat.

BETTY: Oh, Enid . . .

LINDA: Well, I'd sooner set foot in a piranha-infested swamp . . .

BETTY: Hey, why don't you two meet round here when Jim's working late?

ENID: Look at this eh, Carol. See what this lark's set off. Betty's now into bloody communes. Where will it end?

LINDA: Sounds like a good idea to me.

BETTY: Trouble is with you, Enid. You're afraid of change.

ENID: See! She's even talking like one of them. Next we know she'll be wearing an afghan.

LINDA (*eyebrows raised*): Mum.

ENID (*smiles*): It's a dog's life.

BETTY: Wednesday evenings, Jim always works late.

LINDA: What d'you say?

ENID: I reckon it's like a bloody James Bond film just ter see me own daughter. Shall we wear a red carnation?

LINDA (*gets up to go*): Meet you by the lift at seven . . . I've got to go now.

CAROL: How are you getting home?

LINDA: Bus. (*Slight pause. She smiles.*) It's a bit cold for a cross-country run.

CAROL: I'll give you a lift if you want.

LINDA: Ta. See yer . . .

ENID: Take care, love.

CAROL: Bye Mum, Enid.

LINDA *and* CAROL *go out.*

BETTY: Listen, Enid, we ain't ever going to get in this sort of mess again, right?

ENID: From now on whatever spills outta Jim or Bob's mouth we take no notice.

BETTY: We make up our own minds.

ENID (*pause*): Your Carol seemed a bit quiet.

BETTY: I don't really think she's very happy.

ENID: But she's got everything she wanted. She thinks she's got problems, could've turned out like our Linda.

BETTY: It was strange seeing them both together. Linda seems so much younger so full of life . . . I don't know . . .

ENID (*pause*): God, sometimes I could kill Bob.

BETTY: Huh, you're always claiming that when they made him they broke the mould.

ENID: It was obviously cracked already, if you ask me. It don't do going on about it but today, Betty, he was out of order . . . really out of order.

BETTY: They must really rub each other up the wrong way.

ENID: He's only got ter ketch sight of her and he starts up. An' yer know something, Betty, it was really good of her ter come over here, Christ knows how long this carry-on would have lasted. (*Pause.*) Come to think, how the hell did she know about it?

BETTY: Well, don't look at me.

ENID: An' Bob wouldn't ave told her, that's fer sure.

BETTY: Strange like, the bond between mother and daughter, yer know, Enid.

ENID: Oh Gawd, Betty, don't go all psychic on me an' all. That's all I need.

Scene Eleven

12 December 1982. Four a.m. LINDA *and* FIONA *dressed in dark clothing have just completed spraying a sex shop.*

LINDA (*stands back to admire her work. Makes a gesture with her hand*): Bellissimo.

FIONA: Come on let's get outta here.

LINDA: What do you think of it?

FIONA: Wonderful. Come on, make sure you've not left any evidence.

LINDA: Oh yeah, didn't I tell you? I've sprayed, 'I did it really' on your back.

FIONA: Very funny. Leave the can and let's get out.

They start walking.

LINDA: Just as well you let me do it. We'd have been here till the bloody shop opened, the polemic you wanted to inscribe.

FIONA: Save your breath. We might get a few hours' kip if we're lucky.

LINDA: You know something, your spelling is a discredit to your sex.

FIONA: As long as that's the only thing, I'm laughing.

Both smile and FIONA *puts her arm round* LINDA.

FIONA: Er, oh. (*She lets her arm drop.*)

LINDA: Tomorrow's bacon has made an appearance.

A POLICE CONSTABLE *enters.*

POLICE CONSTABLE: Good morning, ladies.

FIONA: Morning, officer.

POLICE CONSTABLE: What, may I ask, are you two girls doing out alone this late or early should I say?

FIONA: We were er . . . just admiring Hackney's architecture silhouetted against the dawn skyline.

LINDA (*mumbles*): Huh, ketch me admiring no phallic symbols I don't think.

POLICE CONSTABLE (*looking at watch*): What dawn?

FIONA: Moon. Against the pale glow of the moon.

LINDA: Winter solstice.

FIONA *stifles a laugh.*

POLICE CONSTABLE: Been to a party then?

FIONA: Yes.

POLICE CONSTABLE: Not thinking of driving I hope.

LINDA (*mimes turning a steering wheel*): No, just pretending.

POLICE CONSTABLE: Don't try and be funny with me, Miss.

FIONA: We left our car. We thought it best to walk.

POLICE CONSTABLE: Very advisable. Not on a yellow line I trust.

FIONA: No a private road.

POLICE CONSTABLE: Glad to hear it. Good morning.

POLICE CONSTABLE *goes out.*

LINDA: Morning all. Have a nice day.

FIONA: Shush.

LINDA (*warmly*): No officer, yes officer we parked our non-existent car up a lamp post, officer.

FIONA: Tut, Winter Solstice.

LINDA: Dawn skyline.

FIONA: When we get round the corner we run right? Cos he'll be about to view your handiwork any minute now.

LINDA: S'okay. It's open to the public.

FIONA: You're so cool.

LINDA: He won't even notice it. Thick as shit. (*Then:*) For fuck's sake run.

Scene Twelve

Later the same day. BETTY's *living-room.* BETTY *and* IVY. JIM *enters.*

BETTY: Jim?

JIM (*irritated*): What is it, Betty? I'm late for work.

BETTY: Have you . . . I mean, would it . . .?

JIM: Spit it out.

BETTY: I was wondering . . .

JIM: For Christ's sake, woman, I haven't got all day . . .

BETTY: . . . if I could lend ten quid off next week's housekeeping.

JIM: What? Now?

BETTY: Oh no next Christmas. What d'you think?

JIM: For what?

BETTY: Shopping.

JIM: Shopping? Betty, my love, it's Sunday. The poxy shops are shut.

BETTY: Not all of them.

JIM: You never go shopping on a Sunday.

BETTY: Well . . . I was thinking of popping out . . . for some fresh air.

JIM: Things are bad, Betty, but they ain't that bad. Fresh air don't cost a tenner.

BETTY: I meant . . . fresh air, not a lung-load of lorry fumes . . .

JIM: What? Where have you got to go . . .

BETTY: Er . . . Our Carol's . . .

JIM: They got an air filter in Islington then?

BETTY: Please Jim . . .

JIM: That don't cost ten quid.

BETTY: Five then, could I have five . . .?

JIM: Blimey, Betty, since when did it cost a fiver to git to Carol's? And anyhow if they want you to babysit they can give you a lift there and back.

BETTY: Jim, I would like five quid.

JIM: I daresay we all would. (*He looks at his watch.*) But not until you tell me why and you'd better be quick about it.

BETTY: I'm your wife.

IVY: For God's sake, Betty, tell him, stand up fer yerself.

BETTY: Keep outta this, Mum.

JIM: Don't tell me let me guess. You both been invited to the Palace (*Pause.*) Well, I gotta go.

BETTY *stands between him and the door.*

BETTY: I want to get a cheap-day return somewhere.

JIM: You'll be getting a one-way ticket to the funny farm if you don't make sense in ten seconds flat.

BETTY: I just thought I'd go for an outing.

JIM: Yeah, I grasped that much but WHERE?

BETTY (*pause. Mumbles*): Newbury.

JIM: Who bury? That rings a bell. Betty a joke's a joke. Now, what do you really want to do?

BETTY: Really, I thought I'd go . . .

JIM: Just knock these daft notions outta yer head once an' fer all. God Almighty, where did you git that idea?

BETTY: I got this letter inviting me.

JIM: Oh, how nice fer you. What did it say. Dear sister Betty, We hear you are a genuine East Ender what actually trod the same pavements as the Pankhursts . . .

BETTY: Jim!

JIM: Don't you Jim me. You'll be right here when I git back. D'you hear me, and we'll sort it out then. I can't waste no more time gabbing about it now.

BETTY: Please . . .

JIM: No way, Betty. No way. Gawd woman, I know you ain't bin hundred per cent lately but it's about time you tried to act normal.

He goes out.

BETTY (*to* IVY): Why did you have to blurt it out?

IVY: He wouldn't have given it to you anyway.

BETTY: No thanks to you. The one time it would have bin welcome and you didn't open your mouth and take sides.

IVY: Waste of time. Git more results reasoning with a brick wall, anyhow I got the money.

BETTY: I can't take it off you.

IVY: Yes you can. And you will, girl. (*She gives her two five-pound notes.*)

BETTY: Ta, Mum, I wish you'd come with me.

IVY: It's brass monkeys out there. It'd finish me off. Shame Enid can't git her act together.

BETTY: I s'pose I'd better git me stuff together.

IVY: Whatever you do, git a move on love.

BETTY (*from the kitchen where she is preparing a packed lunch*): Mum, did you ever get fed up?

IVY: Course I did! Why d'you think I had a different man every week.

BETTY (*sneers*): Humph.

IVY: You never forgave me for that one time, did you?

BETTY: I forgot that incident a long time ago. But you're right, Mum, I never forgave you. I'm sorry, honest. By the way, I've borrowed one of your thermal vests.

Pause.

IVY: I was on the game, Betty. It was the

only way to get money but I'm not making excuses, other women seemed to manage. That night before you came home and he came round to court yer, I'd just shown a fella out and he got the wrong idea. Believe me, because this is the truth. I know I can't call it rape because I was in no position to, everyone would have laughed at me but I did everything I could to stop him. Betty, it was totally against my will. He proved stronger than me.

BETTY: Why didn't you tell me at the time?

IVY: I tried to.

The doorbell rings.

BETTY (*crossing to the door*): Oh, Gawd what now?

IVY: Don't worry, it's probably the *Sunday Times* come to do an exclusive interview.

BETTY (*opening door*): Carol, what are you doing here?

CAROL *enters, looking as though she has been crying.*

CAROL: Oh, were you going out?

BETTY: Well . . . I . . .

IVY: Yes she is.

BETTY: Did you want something, I mean special?

CAROL: No . . . no . . . It doesn't matter.

IVY: Is Darrel with you?

CAROL: No. No.

BETTY: What's he doing?

CAROL: His nut. If you must know, we've run out of Alpen. Well it was the third time this year but the way he went on . . . (*She is on the verge of tears.*) Oh . . . Mum . . .

BETTY (*takes CAROL's hand then starts to take her own coat off*): Come on, tell me what happened.

IVY: Git that coat back on, girl . . . You can both sort it out on the train (*To* CAROL:) Your mother is going to do her bit fer peace. I suggest you go with her while that husband of yours does his pieces in bits, ha ha let him sweat.

CAROL: But what about Joe-Joe?

BETTY: About time Darrel learnt to look after his son for a whole day, don't you think?

CAROL (*pause*): Yes I suppose it bloody well is. All right then.

BETTY: Good. (*Slight pause.*) You know, I think the last thing we did together was buy the material for your wedding dress.

IVY: And it still will be if you two don't get a move on and stop jawing.

The doorbell rings.

CAROL: Oh, God help me, that's probably Darrel.

BETTY (*crossing to the door*): High time you got your own back then. (*She points to the kitchen.*) There's a tin of tomatoes in the cupboard. (*She opens the door.* ENID *enters with a suitcase.*) Enid, you changed your mind?

IVY: Gawd Enid, that must be some packed lunch. What you got in there, half a horse's carcass?

ENID: Didn't you know, Ivy. I just stabbed the rag and bone man to death.

BETTY: Be serious, Enid.

ENID: Just landed the chip pan over bully boy Bob's bonce didn't I.

BETTY: Is he all right?

ENID: Talk sense. When has he ever bin all right?

CAROL: Is he badly hurt?

ENID: Made no difference. No sense. No feeling.

BETTY (*looking at suitcase*): Here, you're not planning to stay down there?

ENID: Do me a favour. I ain't going down there.

IVY: So, what you got in there, Bob or a dented chip pan?

CAROL: She's joking. You're coming with us, aren't you?

ENID: Am I hell!

BETTY: Where the hell are you going then?

ENID: Bognor.

BETTY: *Bognor*! Enid, it's the middle of bloody December.

ENID: I didn't have a stand-up fight with super gut so I could wallow about in mud all day.

IVY: You won't notice the difference on that beach.

BETTY (*to* ENID): That's just typical of you that is. We set this up to do something important fer a change but you, oh no not you. You take the opportunity to enjoy yourself.

CAROL: Don't be too hasty. Who ever enjoyed Bognor?

IVY (*gently*): Knock me down with a feather. Our Carol's made a joke. Quick, write it in your diary.

CAROL (*sharing the moment*): Thank you, Nan.

ENID: Depends what you mean by important. (*To* BETTY:) So you go down there for a day. Right, fine. Come back. Nothing's changed. Big deal.

BETTY: So you go down to Bognor for a day. That's really earth-shattering, I must say.

ENID: Not fer a day, I'm going ter stay wiv me sister.

BETTY: Pardon?

ENID: I've left that stupid big wally.

BETTY: But Enid . . . Enid, what about the children?

ENID: The children? The children are practically fucking geriatric.

BETTY: You can't . . .

ENID: I have, Betty, I have. Bomb or no bomb I got round to thinking I ain't waiting around for it, biding me time stuffing a crew of big-bellied boozers.

IVY: Gawd Almighty, we got a true-life documentary on our hands. At this rate we're all going to feature on *Newsnight*.

BETTY: Carol, say something.

CAROL: Enid, I think you're very brave.

ENID: Ta.

BETTY: Say something positive. You've been watching too many films.

ENID: You won't talk me outta it, Betty.

BETTY: I'm really going ter miss yer.

ENID: You can come down and stay with me.

BETTY: It's not really sunk in.

ENID: I'm going to do something that will change me. You do what you want but I want something more.

BETTY: Huh, you don't want much.

ENID: Not really no. I just don't intend to hang around fer me arms and legs be blown off before I gets round to putting me life in order.

CAROL: I think we should make a move . . .

IVY: Have you got the car, girl?

CAROL: Oh yes.

IVY: In that case I'll git me coat and come with you.

CAROL: Tell you what, Enid, if you come with us, I'll take you on to Bognor.

ENID: Are you sure? It'll make it a ver long day.

CAROL: Oh bugger the Sunday
    dinner.

BETTY: And if we end up in Holloway
    we can bugger the Christmas dinner
    an' all.

to

ry

Methuen Theatrescripts

*published in the Royal Court Writers Series
**screenplays
†published in the RSC Playtexts Series
‡published in the Women's Playhouse Play Series

SAMBA
by Michael Abbensetts
EAST-WEST & IS UNCLE JACK
  A CONFORMIST?
by Audrey Amalrik
*BURIED INSIDE EXTRA
by Thomas Babe
*THE LUCKY CHANCE
by Aphra Behn
DEREK & Choruses from AFTER
  THE ASSASSINATIONS
THE WAR PLAYS:
  PARTS ONE & TWO
  PART THREE
HUMAN CANNON
by Edward Bond
SORE THROATS & SONNETS
  OF LOVE AND
  OPPOSITION
*THE GENIUS
by Howard Brenton
THIRTEENTH NIGHT & A
  SHORT SHARP SHOCK!
by Howard Brenton (*A Short Sharp
  Shock!* written with Tony Howard)
SLEEPING POLICEMEN
by Howard Brenton and Tunde Ikoli
†MOLIÈRE
by Mikhail Bulgakov (in a version by
  Dusty Hughes)
†MONEY
by Edward Bulwer-Lytton
RETURN TO THE FORBIDDEN
  PLANET
by Bob Carlton
*THE SEAGULL
by Anton Chekov (in a version by
  Thomas Kilroy)
SHONA, LUNCH GIRLS, THE
  SHELTER
by Tony Craze, Ron Hart Johnnie
  Quarrell
POOR TOM & TINA
by David Cregan
WRECKERS
TEENDREAMS
ENTERTAINING STRANGERS
by David Edgar
*NEAPTIDE
RIPEN OUR DARKNESS &
  THE DEVIL'S GATEWAY
by Sarah Daniels
†THE BODY
by Nick Darke

TORCH SONG TRILOGY
by Harvey Fierstein
†OUR FRIENDS IN THE NORTH
by Peter Flannery
RUMBLINGS
by Peter Gibbs
THE GOVERNMENT INSPECTOR
by Nikolai Gogol (in a version by
  Adrian Mitchell)
*OTHER WORLDS
*THE OVERGROWN PATH
TODAY
by Robert Holman
*RAT IN THE SKULL
by Ron Hutchinson
†PEER GYNT
by Henrik Ibsen (translated by
  David Rudkin)
*CRIES FROM THE MAMMAL
  HOUSE
*INSIGNIFICANCE
by Terry Johnson
FROZEN ASSETS
SUS
**THE LONG GOOD FRIDAY
BASTARD ANGEL
BETTER TIMES
by Barrie Keeffe
THE 1984 VERITY BARGATE
  AWARD SHORT PLAYS
  (*Up for None* by Mick Mahoney &
  Coming Apart by Melissa Murray)
  Edited by Barrie Keeffe
*NOT QUITE JERUSALEM
by Paul Kember
*BORDERLINE
by Hanif Kureishi
*TOUCHED
*TIBETAN INROADS
THE RAGGED TROUSERED
  PHILANTHROPISTS
MOVING PICTURES
  (*Moving Pictures, Seachange,
  Stars, Strive*)
by Stephen Lowe
PEACE PLAYS
  (*The Fence* by Comman Ground;
  The Celebration of Kokura by
  Berta Freistadt; *Clam* by Deborah
  Levy; *Keeping Body and Soul
  Together* by Stephen Lowe;
  The Tragedy of King Real by
  Adrian Mitchell) Edited by
  Stephen Lowe

PROGRESS & HARD FEELINGS
by Doug Lucie
LAVENDER BLUE & NOLI
  ME TANGERE
by John Mackendrick
**THE PLOUGHMAN'S LUNCH
by Ian McEwan
*EDMOND
by David Mamet
THICK AS THIEVES
WELCOME HOME, RASPBERRY,
THE LUCKY ONES
by Tony Marchant
†A NEW WAY TO PAY OLD
  DEBTS
by Philip Massinger
PLAY MAS, INDEPENDENCE &
  MEETINGS
by Mustapha Matura
LUNATIC AND LOVER
by Michael Meyer
*OPERATION BAD APPLE
*AN HONOURABLE TRADE
by G. F. Newman
REAL ESTATE
‡BEAUTY AND THE BEAST
SALONIKA
by Louise Page
ONE FOR THE ROAD
by Harold Pinter
STRAWBERRY FIELDS
SHOUT ACROSS THE RIVER
AMERICAN DAYS
THE SUMMER PARTY
**FAVOURITE NIGHTS &
  CAUGHT ON A TRAIN
**RUNNERS & SOFT TARGETS
by Stephen Poliakoff
BRIMSTONE AND TREACLE
by Dennis Potter
†THE TIME OF YOUR LIFE
by William Saroyan
‡SPELL NUMBER SEVEN
by Ntozake Shange
*AUNT DAN AND LEMON
MY DINNER WITH ANDRÉ &
MARIE AND BRUCE
by Wallace Shawn (My Dinner with
  André written with André
  Gregory)
HOW THE VOTE WAS WON and
other suffragette plays
an anthology edited by Dale Spender
  and Carole Hayman
LIVE THEATRE: Four Plays for
  Young People
by C. P. Taylor
BAZAAR & RUMMAGE,
GROPING FOR WORDS and
WOMBERANG

*THE GREAT CELESTIAL COW
by Sue Townsend
PLAYS BY WOMEN: VOL 1
(Vinegar Tom by Caryl Churchill;
  Dusa, Fish, Stas and Vi by Pam
  Gems; Tissue by Louise Page;
  Aurora Leigh by Michelene
  Wandor)
PLAYS BY WOMEN: VOL 2
(Trafford Tanzi by Claire Luckham;
  Letters Home by Rose Leiman
  Goldemberg; Rites by Maureen
  Duffy; Find Me by Olwen Wymark)
PLAYS BY WOMEN: VOL 3
(Aunt Mary by Pam Gems; Red Devils
  by Debbie Horsfield; Blood
  Relations by Sharon Pollock;
  Time Pieces by Lou Wakefield and
  The Women's Theatre Group)
PLAYS BY WOMEN: VOL 4
(Objections to Sex and Violence by
  Caryl Churchill: Rose's Story by
  Grace Dayley; Blood and Ice by
  Liz Lochhead; Pinball by Alison
  Lyssa)
Edited by Michelene Wandor
**CITIZEN KANE
by Orson Welles and Herman
  J. Mankiewicz
CLAY
by Peter Whelan
THE NINE NIGHT & RITUAL BY
  WATER
by Edgar White
RENTS
LENT
by Michael Wilcox
GAY PLAYS: VOL 1
(Submariners by Tom McClenaghan;
  The Green Bay Tree by Mordaunt
  Shairp; Passing By by Martin
  Sherman; Accounts by Michael
  Wilcox)
VOL 2 (Quaint Honour by
  Roger Gellert; Bearclaw by
  Timothy Mason; Cracks by Martin
  Sherman; Lies About Vietnam
  by C. P. Taylor)
SUGAR AND SPICE & TRIAL
  RUN
W.C.P.C.
by Nigel Williams
*THE GRASS WIDOW
by Snoo Wilson
HAS 'WASHINGTON' LEGS &
  DINGO
by Charles Wood
THE DESERT AIR
†CUSTOM OF THE COUNTRY
by Nicholas Wright

Methuen's Modern Plays

Bertolt Brecht	*Mother Courage and Her Children*
	The Caucasian Chalk Circle
	The Good Person of Szechwan
	The Life of Galileo
	The Threepenny Opera
	Saint Joan of the Stockyards
	The Resistible Rise of Arturo Ui
	The Mother
	Mr Puntila and His Man Matti
	The Measures Taken and other Lehrstücke
	The Days of the Commune
	The Messingkauf Dialogues
	Man Equals Man and *The Elephant Calf*
	The Rise and Fall of the City of Mahagonny and *The Seven Deadly Sins*
	Baal
	A Respectable Wedding and other one-act plays
	Drums in the Night
	In the Jungle of Cities
	Fear and Misery of the Third Reich and *Señora Carrar's Rifles*
	Schweyk in the Second World War and *The Visions of Simone Machard*

Brecht ⎫
Weill ⎬   *Happy End*
Lane ⎭

Howard Brenton	*The Churchill Play*
	Weapons of Happiness
	Epsom Downs
	The Romans in Britain
	Plays for the Poor Theatre
	Magnificence
	Revenge
	Hitler Dances
	Bloody Poetry

Howard Brenton and David Hare	*Brassneck* *Pravda*
Mikhail Bulgakov	*The White Guard*
Caryl Churchill	*Top Girls* *Fen* and *Softcops*
Noël Coward	*Hay Fever*
Sarah Daniels	*Masterpieces*
Shelagh Delaney	*A Taste of Honey* *The Lion in Love*
David Edgar	*Destiny* *Mary Barnes* *Maydays*
Michael Frayn	*Clouds* *Make and Break* *Noises Off* *Benefactors*
Max Frisch	*The Fire Raisers* *Andorra* *Triptych*
Simon Gray	*Butley* *Otherwise Engaged and other plays* *Dog Days* *The Rear Column and other plays* *Close of Play and Pig in a Poke* *Stage Struck* *Quartermaine's Terms* *The Common Pursuit*
Peter Handke	*Offending the Audience* and *Self-Accusation* *Kaspar* *The Ride Across Lake Constance* *They Are Dying Out*
Kaufman & Hart	*Once in a Lifetime, You Can't Take It With You* and *The Man Who Came To Dinner*
Vaclav Havel	*The Memorandum*

Barrie Keeffe	*Gimme Shelter (Gem, Gotcha, Getaway)*
	Barbarians (Killing Time, Abide With Me, In the City)
	A Mad World, My Masters
Arthur Kopit	*Indians*
	Wings
John McGrath	*The Cheviot, the Stag and the Black, Black Oil*
David Mamet	*Glengarry Glen Ross*
	American Buffalo
David Mercer	*After Haggerty*
	Cousin Vladimir and *Shooting the Chandelier*
	Duck Song
	The Monster of Karlovy Vary and *Then and Now*
	No Limits To Love
Arthur Miller	*The American Clock*
	The Archbishop's Ceiling
	Two-Way Mirror
	Danger! Memory!
Percy Mtwa, Mbongeni Ngema, Barney Simon	*Woza Albert*
Peter Nichols	*Passion Play*
	Poppy
Joe Orton	*Loot*
	What the Butler Saw
	Funeral Games and *The Good and Faithful Servant*
	Entertaining Mr Sloane
	Up Against It
Louise Page	*Golden Girls*
Harold Pinter	*The Birthday Party*
	The Room and *The Dumb Waiter*
	The Caretaker
	A Slight Ache and other plays
	The Collection and *The Lover*
	The Homecoming

Best Radio Plays of 1981 (Peter Barnes:
  The Jumping Mimuses of Byzantium;
  Don Haworth: *Talk of Love and War:*
  Harold Pinter: *Family Voices;* David
  Pownall: *Beef:* J P Rooney: *The Dead
  Image;* Paul Thain: *The Biggest
  Sandcastle in the World*)
Best Radio Plays of 1982 (Rhys
  Adrian:*Watching the Plays Together;*
  John Arden: *The Old Man Sleeps
  Alone;* Harry Barton: *Hoopoe Day;*
  Donald Chapman: *Invisible Writing;*
  Tom Stoppard: *The Dog It Was
  That Died;* William Trevor: *Autumn
  Sunshine*)
Best Radio Plays of 1983 (Wally K Daly:
  Time Slip; Shirley Gee: *Never in My
  Lifetime;* Gerry Jones: *The Angels They
  Grow Lonely;* Steve May: *No
  Exceptions;* Martyn Read: *Scouting for
  Boys*)
Best Radio Plays of 1984 (Stephen
  Dunstone: *Who Is Sylvia?;* Don
  Haworth: *Daybreak;* Robert Ferguson:
  Transfigured Night; Caryl Phillips:
  The Wasted Years; Christopher Russell:
  Swimmer; Rose Tremain: *Temporary
  Shelter*)

KING ALFRED'S COLLEGE
LIBRARY

113055 T
4/7/88
A.B.P